World War 1

The Story of Air Combat in World War 1

(WWI True Story of Smuggling Guns to the Irish Coast)

Sherry Lucas

Published By **Bengion Cosalas**

Sherry Lucas

All Rights Reserved

World War 1: The Story of Air Combat in World War 1 (WWI True Story of Smuggling Guns to the Irish Coast)

ISBN 978-1-77485-725-0

No part of this guidebook shall be reproduced in any form without permission in writing from the publisher except in the case of brief quotations embodied in critical articles or reviews.

Legal & Disclaimer

The information contained in this ebook is not designed to replace or take the place of any form of medicine or professional medical advice. The information in this ebook has been provided for educational & entertainment purposes only.

The information contained in this book has been compiled from sources deemed reliable, and it is accurate to the best of the Author's knowledge; however, the Author cannot guarantee its accuracy and validity and cannot be held liable for any errors or omissions. Changes are periodically made to this book. You must consult your doctor or get professional medical advice before using any of the suggested remedies, techniques, or information in this book.

Upon using the information contained in this book, you agree to hold harmless the Author from and against any damages, costs, and expenses, including any legal fees potentially resulting from the application of any of the information provided by this guide. This disclaimer applies to any damages or injury caused by the use and application, whether directly or indirectly, of any advice or information presented, whether for breach of contract, tort, negligence, personal injury, criminal intent, or under any other cause of action.

You agree to accept all risks of using the information presented inside this book. You need to consult a professional medical practitioner in order to ensure you are both able and healthy enough to participate in this program.

TABLE OF CONTENTS

Introduction 1

Chapter 1: Preparation For The Global Conflagration 6

Chapter 2: The First Strike: Schlieffen Has A Plan 13

Chapter 3: The War Is The Eastern Front Is Not So Quiet On The Eastern Front 18

Chapter 4: "Down In The Trenches 24

Chapter 5: Britain Bombed By Zeppelin . 29

Chapter 6: Surviving The Storm In Russia 34

Chapter 7: Allied March On The Ottoman Empire 38

Chapter 8: The Battle Of Verdun 47

Chapter 9: The Great Russian Rebound . 52

Chapter 10:, America Is A Participant In Into War For The Allies 56

Chapter 11: Italy Under Siege 61

Chapter 12: The Great Russian Collapse 67

Chapter 13: The Turkish Battle Of Armageddon 73

Chapter 14: Germany Loses The War..... 78

Chapter 15: Europe And The World In 1914 91

Chapter 16: The Progress Of The War 1915- 1916.. 124

Conclusion 181

Introduction

It's amazing how few people are aware of the events that started World War One. Even for those who know a bit more about the war, it's awe-inspiring how seemingly minor incidents can result in a massive firestorm. The archduke was killed at the age of 58 in Sarajevo, Bosnia, by an individual who was influenced by a terrorist group from Serbia. Austria-Hungary became furious with Serbia as did Serbia's allies Russia was then angry with Austria as Austria's allies Germany turned on Russia as did France and England began to be angry with Germany. The dominoes were started through the death of the archduke. But was it actually this particular incident that ignited the fire in the beginning of World War One?

The answer is yes or no. It was, in fact, an assassin's bullet slicing through an Austrian official, which accelerated the demands for war, however, to assert that this single incident was the only reason could be a falsehood, given that there were multiple layers of complexity brewing beneath the surface during that time. However, to fully understand the context to World War One, you must understand the political context of where the flame was ignited. That's why you need to be familiar the tense political events that occurred in the Balkans between the 15th century through the early 20th century.

After a long period of intrusion In 1463, The Ottoman Turks stormed into Bosnia and joined it into their empire. Over the next few period the fortunes of the Ottoman Empire would fluctuate and fall until Turkish expansion into the Balkans was halted decisively in 1699 with the Treaty of Karlowitz. Following the defeat of what was known as the Holy League, a conglomeration of European powers (the Hapsburg Empire, Poland-Lithuania, Venice, and Russia) the Ottomans were obliged to surrender a large portion of their territories located in western Balkans and from that point onwards, they would not advance further. After the surrender of this region, Bosnia became the farthest frontier of the Ottoman Empire.

Awed by the major victory over their Turkish oppressors, Bosnian freedom fighters would remain sporadic in their resistance to Ottoman rule throughout the rest of the century and culminated in the massive uprising that began in 1875. The conflict grew increasingly heated, Serbia and Russia became involved and joined forces in battle against their former foe the Ottomans. In the midst of its decline and already severely weakened it was a matter of time before the Ottoman Empire suffered a defeat. The latest defeat resulted in 1878's Congress of Berlin, which was a bid to settle the outcomes of the war.

All the Bosnians desired was their own independence however, even with victory over the Ottomans their natural rights was still denied to Bosnians. They were able to decide that a different foreign power - this time, Austria-Hungary - would govern the region. The Bosnians didn't rise up in opposition to the Ottoman Empire in order to be taken over in the Austro-Hungarian Empire but this is exactly what transpired. In 1908, the rule of law which Austria-Hungary was given was made permanent after Bosnia and Herzegovina was officialy annexed to Austro-Hungarians.

The freedom of speech was repressed however, in the wake of the underground movements bent to overthrow Austrian rule started popping everywhere. The one of them dubbed its self "the Black Hand." To be precise this, the Black Hand originated in Bosnia and was actually based in Serbia. Its Serbian Nationalists who were part who were part of"the Black Hand, however, were equally dissatisfied with Austro-Hungarians taking control of Balkan properties, believing that they were hindering the development of a "Greater Serbia" of which Bosnia could have been an integral part.

This was because it was the Black Hand that "sponsored" an attack on austro-hungarian dignitaries in 1914, an attack in which teenager Bosnian murderer Gavrilo Princip would take on the main part. By chance, 19-year-old Gavrilo was in the right spot (or perhaps stated in the wrong location) when he was in the proper place at the appropriate moment and was able shoot a straight shot at the visitor Archduke Franz Ferdinand as his car drove through.

After being detained and brought before a jury, Gavrilo would maintain that it was just a libertarian trying to break free from the burden of an oppressive power. Whatever else can be discussed on the subject, it was the beliefs and actions of this assassin that caused World War One, but as the above passages show that there was a dark and sinister presence in the background that led the world towards this horrific tipping point. It's not just limited to the terrorist organization as well as the dark hand of human avarice jealousy, and resentment in general which fueled the hellish fires that started to burn at the beginning.

Chapter 1: Preparation For The Global Conflagration

While German-speaking people have existed for hundreds many years, however, the present Germany that we know today was not a reality until the late 19th century. Germany as is today have its beginnings until end of the 19th century. Before that, various combinations of German power were gone such as The Holy Roman Empire, Prussia and in part The Austro-Hungarian Empire. However, it was the newly unification of the German state (taking about the same amount of land like it does today) was at the heart of a massive arms buildup that was to spread across the whole European continent and further.

When Germany first became famous after the conclusion in the French-Prussian War, in 1871 and Kaiser Wilhelm was inaugurated to become the very first "German Emperor." Indeed, prior to the defeat of Germany in World War One, the young German nation was known by the name of German Empire. The first German Emperor was instrumental in establishing the known as the "League of Three Kings" comprised three countries:

Austria-Hungary, Russia, and Germany. This alliance was brief but it was a failure. It was a failure when Austria-Hungary and Russia were at odds over their opposing opinions about how the next steps for the Balkans should look like.

The rift pushed Russia away from the German orbit, and led Austria-Hungary along with Germany to join forces in a more tense alliance. At the time the Kaiser Wilhelm II came into his position and in power, it was clear that the future of Germany and Austria-Hungary could not be separated. Whatever happened to one would invariably impact the other. Germany is, in its own way was the first stronghold of Europe that was blessed with a wealth of mineral riches and a the capacity to manufacture at full. The most significant flaw in the stars of Germany however, was the fragility of its political system.

In contrast to older counterparts like Britain and France in the early days, the German nation was still trying to identified the kind of social contract it wanted to be part of. German democracy was splintered at worst and the autocratic character of the Kaiser made the country an extreme stance from the start. Despite the quasi-democratic nature of the Reichstag but ultimately, it that the Kaiser held the final say on matters of foreign policy and, most importantly, the decision to declare war. This will be crucial in the German reaction in the lead-up up to World War One.

Germany in the meantime was trying to get involved in international affairs with the policy known as Weltpolitik which in English signifies World Politics. Through international intervention as well as extraterritorial land grabs this strategy of Weltpolitik could eventually bring about confrontation with German nation's European counterparts. Of all the two, France was the most likely to strike back if it was pushed. France had, after all was already humiliated by the newly formed German people at close of the Franco-Prussian war in the 1870s in the beginning.

France had lost a significant territory during this war (the Alsace-Lorraine region along the West bank of Rhine) in the very creation of the new German nation. This is why, and much more, at the period of World War One a few years after, France was more than ready to settle the issue.

However, of all the great powers that could be dragged into the firestorm of the First World War, Russia's role was the least certain. Russia has long been regarded as an enormous power of Europe due to its size, population, and a powerful army.

For the majority of the in the early and mid 20th century, Russia was a power that was in decline. In terms of economics, Russia was a mess and it was France who helped keep Russian finances going with frequent loans and investments in the faltering Russian infrastructure. However, despite being on the brink of collapse Russia was a bold and ambitious country in addition which led directly to the Balkans by a strategy that was known as "Pan-Slavism." It was the "Slavs," you see are an old eastern European group which Russia as well as many of the Balkan states are part of.

It was Russia's plan early in the process to help (if not to subjugate) the country's Balkan neighbors, like Bosnia as well as Herzegovina. Russia played the role of the great guardian , protector and protector of its neighbors Slavic states. Should the Western powers started to move towards them with a vengeance, Russia would inevitably feel it was compelled to run to help. Because of all the above conditions, though Austria-Hungary as well as Bosnia-Herzegovina were the main actors but it was France, Germany, and Russia with the highest of the stakes.

Britain was a unlikely ally for the French was a major participant with a vested desire in these matters also, because it was worried that a revived Germany could become a serious threat against Britain. British Empire. For the British the main objective from the beginning of World War One was to maintain the status quo in control. Less powerful powers, on contrary, like those who were referred to as the "sick guy from Europe" (the fast decreasing Ottoman Empire) had been trying to escape their current status quo and, by taking a gamble with Germany during the early stages of World War One, the Ottomans were hoping to win back the territory they lost.

They were the primary pieces on the chessboard for the political realm before the beginning of World War One. With all the key players in place The onset of World War One occurred as follows. The first was that

Archduke Franz Ferdinand, visiting from Austria was killed. Following the assassination the angry Austria demanded Serbia (the nation that the terrorist group responsible for the attack, known as the "Black Hand" was a member of) to comply with 10 demands that were draconian in order to avoid an all-out conflict. For the Serbians the most urgent of these demands was to accept the appointment of "representatives from the Austro-Hungarian state to thwart subversive groups."

Serbia along with its allies believed that a stern request for foreign interference in their own government was equivalent to suicide, and they ultimately decided to decline. Austria-Hungary was, however, aware that Serbia is likely to reject their demands, was in private talks with Germany which assured it of that it would support Austria-Hungary regardless of the outcome. Also known as the "blank checks" in the document that Germans gave to the Austrians and it was this assurance of Germany's military might that inspired the Austro-Hungarians in their attempt to force Serbia into conflict.

As a result, in the event that demands from Austria were not fulfilled On the 25th of July in 1914 Austria-Hungary announced war against Serbia and troops from Austro-Hungary began to move towards the border. The next step was mobilisation by Russian troops throughout the region as a reaction to the war that was being waged against its ally, Serbia. The moment this took place, Germany demanded that Russia be halted, and issued them an ultimatum that they must limit their troops within 12 hours.

Russia was, naturally, was not willing to sign such a treaty and, as a result on August 1, Germany declared war on Russia. The following day, the Germans concluded a treaty Russia's ancestors and the Ottoman Empire which brought the long-standing Islamic empire into the conflict with Germany. The Germans were then able to demand that France remain out of the war however France did not agree, which led to Germany declaring war against France and this led to each of Britain in addition to France declaring war against Germany. Just like that, World War One had begun.

Chapter 2: The First Strike: Schlieffen Has A Plan

Prior to the time that World War One occurred, the German military had a plan of contingency in place, in the event that it was required to fight on two fronts , namely France as well as Russia. It was known by"the "Schlieffen Plan" this strategy came from the concept from general Alfred von Schlieffen in the early 20th century. Schlieffen had dreamed of the scenario that Germany was in danger of being attacked coming from France and Russia and left German soldiers with a ratio of five to three. This was not a good chances to consider and Schlieffen came up with strategies to stop it.

In this case Schlieffen believed it was essential to Germany to deliver a decisive strike to France first, so that the full German force could be drawn up in the eastern region to take out Russia. The most difficult aspect of this plan was the fortifications that French had erected at the border between France and Germany but Schlieffen believed that the German army could just ignore these fortifications, but instead openly infringe on the neutrality of neighbouring Holland,

Belgium, and Luxembourg. In sending soldiers through the areas and further to Northern France, Germany avoided the wall that divides west and east border between France and Germany completely.

The first effort to bypass of French defenses was made using French defenses. The German First as well as Second Armies, which stormed through Belgium and drove straight to Northern France. Its Third Army then passed right through the Belgian Ardennes and was following by Fifth and Fourth armies marching across Luxembourg as well as through the French Ardennes. These were only a few out of the 69 divisions Germany deployed in World War One with a fighting force of 2292,000 at the peak.

The German military would clash with France in the first battles of the war, in what was later referred to in"the "Battle of Frontiers." The Germans were initially ahead however French troops, bolstered through British Expeditionary Force British Expeditionary Force (which had just been sent out) were not easily defeated and were able defend themselves - in an attempt to prepare for the trench war, they literally got "entrenched."

The result was the resulting standoff that would be"the "First Battle of Marne." It began in the Western Front on September 6th 1914 and proved to be a huge disappointment and a first setback for the Germans.

In a state of denial, the German divisions that were positioned in this region of Northern France quickly became outnumbered and isolated as more French divisions came in through Southern France. In this trap and trapped, it was the German First Army tried to break free of its predicament, before facing with the French Sixth Army, but when they did so, they was able to widen the gap in between First as well as the Second German armies. The resulting division led to the German top command concerned about an imminent break-up of the unification German Front, in September 9, a total retreat was ordered to that River Aisne, to the east.

When the Germans left as the Germans fled, the Allies were digging into their trenches and, by the 14th of September, had created a militarized zone that extended from Switzerland up to the Aisne that was where French trenches would be matched against German trenches, thereby beginning the gruelling process of the trench warfare on the Western Front. The result was deemed to be to be so devastating to Germans that Germans that the commander in charge general Helmuth von Moltke, was fired for his inability to perform. The Kaiser then changed his cabinet, and appointed the general Erich von Falkenhayn to the helm at the place of Moltke.

Following this arrangement the fighting recommenced in that Belgian town Ypres. It was a town that for Ypres did not have any significance but for all those who were involved, it was a place that served as a suitable gateway for troop movements. From here from where German troops launched a massive attack on Belgian as well as French forces, pushing them towards the Yser River. The Germans achieved great success but were faced with an unanticipated danger when the Belgians have opened the flood gates of a dam, which forced the Germans to rush to a retreat against the rising floodwater.

There was a time when the Germans became temporarily stranded on the opposite side of the lake. The conflict that followed. The fighting was so intense that, by the 31st of

October 1914 The German divisions were reduced to only 14,000 soldiers. In the midst of the war, it was clear that the Western Front now stretched all across Switzerland all the way to and including the North Sea. In the wake of this shocking loss, it became clear that the Schlieffen Plan had been an complete fail.

Chapter 3: The War Is The Eastern Front Is Not So Quiet On The Eastern Front

A lot has been written concerning what happened on the Western Front throughout World War One, and the brutal trench warfare in it has become the subject of legend. However, equally dramatic events were taking place in the Eastern Front as well. Russia in the end was a vast country and at any time, it was able to mobilize a standing army of more than 150,000. When it came to compulsory conscription, this number could increase to five million. In aiding the mobilization of Russian forces was that France had made huge investments into its Russian railway system prior to the outbreak of war. That meant as much up to two million Russian soldiers could be placed in train cars and transported into battle with ease.

In the early stages of World War One, the first major battlefield was Poland in Poland, in which Poland was where the Russian First Army faced off against the German Eighth Army. In the midst of this battle it was the Russian army first made a move, and tried to advance on the 16th of August in 1914. In the subsequent battle and lasted for a while, it was reported that on the 20th of August both Russians as well as the Germans had suffered more than 17,000 casualties. It's an unfortunate fact of war to add up the dead to determine who emerged with the most points, but according to this savage calculation it would be possible for the war been deemed as a draw.

The following major battle was not what it seemed. The battle was dubbed"the "Battle of Tannenberg" this war between the Germans and Russians took place between August 26th to the 30th of August. The war was actually triggered through a call that was intercepted by on the part of the Russians through the Germans that received the latest information about Russian troop movements directly from their general Alexander Samsonov himself. To illustrate how chaotic Russian military entry to war was, it appears that they were very lax when it came to encryption for their phone calls.

This kind of mistake could result in some devastating consequences for this Russian army, because it enabled the Germans to bolster their positions and plan an advance to thwart Russian troop movements. The

Germans focused on the Russians precisely where they were they were able to block them with their Russian Second Army, trapping them in the forest near The Polish city of Allenstein. In this battle, Russians were devastated with more than 78,000 people killed and 92,000 being captured. However the Germans only lost around 13,000 soldiers that day.

The most significant aspect of the defeat Russia received during the Battle of Tannenberg is the fact that it required 60 trains to transport all Russian prisoners of the war. At the end, around 10,000 Russian survivors made it out without injury. Russian general Alexander Samsonov paid a high price. It is believed that in a state of denial, and unable to take the pain of his loss He fled into the forest of darkness in the region on his own, in which he decided to commit suicide. himself to the grave, by hitting himself on the head.

In the exact moment that Samsonov was handed this devastating loss, fighting was raging across the area in that was part of the Eastern Front known as "Austria Galicia." This war broke out on August 18th , when Russian troops took to the offensive, advancing towards Austro-Hungarian troops on the plains, in a manner reminiscent of cavalry battles of earlier in the Middle Ages. Instead of armed with lances and broadswords the two sides charged forward, launching the rapid fire of machine guns. The result was horrific for both sides with thousands upon thousands of soldiers being shot down by a relentless assault of artillery shells and bullets.

In the midst tragedy and devastation, the Russians however were able to advance, in September 3, they they managed to take over that city Lemberg and regain control of an important train station. After the takeover however, the Austrians were forced to withdraw, and by September 11, they were pulled back towards the San River. By this time it was evident that they Austrians have already lost 225,000 soldiers. Germany realized it was evident that Austro-Hungary Empire wasn't strong enough to withstand such losses, sought to help the Austrians by forming an "New Ninth Army" and sending it in as an important reinforcement.

The combined force began to attack Russian forces in Poland and extending into the Polish interior before October. However, these gains were quickly reversed on the 18th of October which was when German forces were Germans were forced to retreat that brought back 7 miles west from Warsaw. The Austrians faced the same sort of reverse when, on the 9th of October they managed to regain their former position near their old position along the San River and the Polish city of Przemysl and then be forced back shortly afterward.

The Russians began to attack again in the middle of November, however, the Germans had already been warned off to their imminent arrival. Soldiers from the German Ninth Army were rushed to the frontlines of the battle enough to attack the right side and the right flank of Russian advance. In the flurry of attacks, the Russians were forced away from the centre of Lodz. At one point, the Germans appeared to be ready to take Warsaw but the tide changed so they were defeated. Germans were the first to be repelled. The Russians constructed trenches on the western bank of the Vistula river, which was the place they planned to establish their case.

The Germans were not willing to surrender but at the beginning of December 1914 they were fighting back against the Russians and capturing Przemysl on the 6th of December. As the constant changes can be seen, in contrast to the static stalemate that grew during the initial stages of the Western Front, the Eastern Front was flexible in character. A side could gain ground and then lose ground within a couple of weeks. The frantic battles that continued to rage It was not peaceful at all on the Eastern Front.

Chapter 4: "Down In The Trenches

For most of us trench warfare is most likely what first pops into our thoughts when thinking about the incidents of World War One. There is a reason why that is the case, as from 1914 until 1917, trench conflict in the Western Front was indeed an all-encompassing feature of the war. For the Germans they did not believe that this was the way they wanted things to unfold. The German military's objective was to plow through France with a blitzkrieg-style attack, destroying French out of the war. French off the battlefield within a couple of weeks.

Though this tactic worked in the case of Hitler's Nazis during World War Two, when the tanks were sent to destroy across Western Europe, in World War One the German drives sank in the treacherous trenches. In 1915 The Kaiser as well as his senior advisors were already astonished that their war machine were grinding to the ground, to the point that they considered all sorts of unorthodox strategies to lift themselves from the slumber.

This inclination would eventually lead to the first chemical weapons on the field. On the

22nd April 1915, during the Second Battle of Ypres which was a battle in the Ypres region, The German Fourth Army struck out on Allied posts, while simultaneously firing more than 168 tons of chlorine gas alongside conventional shelling. The effects were immediate. The Allied troops were immediately struck. The gas burnt the eyes, scorched their lung which caused the troops to choke, gag and cough up blood.

Unable to fight back in these conditions, the gassed French soldiers escaped right from the trenches screaming. A lot of the afflicted souls were later shot by Germans. In the gruesome situation, Canadian troops saved the day with members of the First Canadian Division rushing in to defend their troops from the brutal attack.

According to various chroniclers of conflict, this single Canadian division could be one of the most unnoticed heroes of the conflict. According to one historian, "a catastrophe was averted only through the greatest effort, and most importantly the unflinching determination and strength of Canadians. Without a pause, the Canadians were swarmed by deadly gasses, torn by frightening cannonading and surrounded by guns of heavy weight, fought with awe-inspiring odds."

After the confusion of the gas attacks, the Germans were able to almost create an opening in the Allied lines however they were stopped by the First Canadian Division boldly charged into the gap, stopping the collapse of the entire line. The Germans attempted to repeat the same tactics on April 24 however, this time with the Canadians. They were savagely attacked however they were able to stand their positions. Though all sides were aware the possibility of using poison gas, nobody thought that any nation would descend to the point of actually employ it.

In the beginning, German usage of the poison gas in clear violation of the rules for war that were made in the Hague Convention of 1907. But once the Germans set the decision to use it as a precedent that they set, the Allies including the British specifically began to react by launching chemical warfare from their very own. This was the Battle of Loos on September 25th, 1915 that the Brits truly unleashed their chemical arsenal against the Germans.

In the course of this battle, both British and French determinedly tried to break through German lines that surrounded those French cities that were Artois as well as Champagne. However, even with the help of chemical weapons, the battle was largely failed and the British deaths were more than double that of Germans who were killed in the battle. The British were able to make a bold move in the direction of urging their troops from the trenches and out into open terrain. But their bold run exposed them to a continuous assault by German shots.

The mission turned out to be like live soldiers in the meat grinder. The results were not exactly as they British high command was hoping to observe. However it was a success for the British were able to break through the German line of defense and captured the town of Loos-en-Gohelle. The following day however they were able to secure the town. Germans closed off the gap and took the British back.

Another incident which was a testimony to the massive, pointless destruction that was the norm throughout World War One, after thousands of deaths were claimed The warring sides were almost exactly where they started. As in a football match both side simply moved a few yards in order to be tackled by their foes once more. Then, on September 28 the two sides were being retreated back to the same trenches that they had left just a few days earlier. Unfortunately, it was simply another day into the trenches.

Chapter 5: Britain Bombed By Zeppelin

In the year 1914, at the close of the war, Britain was already becoming tired of the misery of trench combat. Every day, the conflict seemed to drag along without any real improvement or significant development. However, the Germans certainly ensured that the British start the new year off with the best of intentions. On the evening of 15th, 1915 Germany set the record straight by launching the first airstrikes ever on London.

The Germans' World War One attacks on London did not employ winged aircraft to drop bombs, but instead used zeppelins that were filled with hydrogen. Zeppelins, which are a massive high-flying car, was invented in the year 1900 by German engineer and officer in the military, Ferdinand Graf von Zeppelin. They were originally designed as an ocean liner to provide entertainment for all the citizens of the world. Ferdinand's first creation is one that was a symbol of peace not war. However, once it was transformed into an anti-bomb platform, the Zeppelin turned out to be an extremely lethal weapon.

The method of delivering the explosives was quite primitive and they were dropped by hand over an opening in the trapdoor, but they could rain down destruction and death all the same. In 20 minutes, the Zeppelins spewed over 3000 pounds of explosives sparking massive fires, and transforming businesses, homes and shops into rubble and killing seven.

It's important to mention that there was not a real motive for the military in the random attack. They were primarily targeted at civilians with no particular military objective in the mind of. The main purpose of these attacks was to scare and terrorize the British to pull their troops from frontlines and ending the conflict. The German leader, Kaiser Wilhelm was initially against the use of zeppelins. His commanders who were less scrupulous were said to have demanded the use of the zeppelins almost immediately however the reason why that it took the Germans over a year bring in the zeppelins was due to the Kaiser's dislike of their usage.

The Kaiser was initially convinced it would be finished in a short time without having to resort to these terror tactics. He was also shocked by the random way the zeppelin destroyed its targets. Wilhelm who was close with the royals of England, was worried that these attacks could destroy the cultural heritage of London. The Kaiser tried to block using these massive helium bombs but, in 1915, his arguments were rejected. The underlings of the Kaiser had decided it was now a good idea to employ the weapons to scare the British to surrender.

The initial attacks targeted primarily civilians in residential areas, which included an entertainment hall, train station and a couple of churches. It was a minor incident in the overall picture, but it caused some fear among the population regardless. One of the most worrying issues to British citizens was that the British was the massive fires that the bombings caused. However, soon enough, the emergency personnel were in a position reduce the harm caused.

Through these random attacks, the Germans were hoping to intimidate the British to surrender their fight against them, but in the midst these terrifying attacks they were met with a resounding victory by the British displayed their determination. The air raid shelters constructed to guard civilians from harm, and, soon after the most effective method for attacking the zeppelins was developed.

For as terrifying as they could have looked in the air they were an extremely vulnerable aerial platform. Once a reliable method to target them was devised it was a matter of playing to blow them up. The balloons contained extremely flammable hydrogen and even a tiny pinprick could be disastrous for the Germans aboard.

British Air defenses at the beginning of their development However they had a basic system of searchlights with high beams which could search the skies as well as a handful of powerful anti-aircraft guns was required to take down the German Zeppelins. If the zeppelins were able to escape these defenses, the British could dispatch a few of their biplanes in the air to pursue them.

When the Zeppelins that previously ruled the air were seen at last, they appeared. British skies were lit with a bright ring as air raid sirens boomed to alert the people below. Anti-aircraft guns continuously launched their rockets into the skies as British aircrafts rushed to chase the balloons back to earth. In the late autumn of 1916, the threat of zeppelins had been effectively eliminated. Finally the stiff lower lip of British was able to prevail over the air-filled beasts that were the work of German engineering.

Chapter 6: Surviving The Storm In Russia

In 1915 the principal German and Russian front lines were located near the Baltic Sea. There, Russian forces comprise two principal parts, the Northern army as well as the Southern army. The Northern army was the fighting force that was located near the East Prussian border, whereas the Southern army was based at the Nareb and within the vicinity of Warsaw. German forces, in contrast were stationed in an area known as the "bending frontier" that was Eastern Prussia, as well as around Ravka and Bzura and were positioned in the front of Warsaw.

The setting was made for what would later be called"the "Winter Battle of the Masurian Lakes." The Masurian Lakes was the region that was located in the northeastern region of Poland in which the battle lines were drawn. In this battle, Germans in the midst of snow falling in heavy fall were able to drive straight through Russian territory. Russian camp, taking the Russians completely off guard. It was the Eighth as well as the Tenth german armies under the direction by General Hindenburg was capable of slicing through Russian army.

In mid-January, the Russians began to form a group and attacked into the valleys of Hungary And by January 17th, the famous Kirlibaba Pass was in their control. The Germans however are more determined than before before to capture Warsaw and they forced their Russians to a savage explosion of artillery at the beginning of February. This first attack was able to take them past Russian lines and , by February 2 they were in the advanced stages of a constant advance.

However, the Russians returned with a revenge and on February 8th they were into Bzura. On February 23 it was the time that the Germans were actually forced to leave their fortifications close to their fortifications to the east of Nieman River. However, by March 8 that day, the Germans were back in the same direction and launched a fierce assault against the Russians. The Russian army didn't expect to see the invading Germans to suddenly turn and launch a volley of attack, as they did, and they were caught out of their element.

The German campaign continued until the Germans could be found behind Russian lines in the vicinity of towns like Pilviszki, Marjampol, Suwalki and Augustof. The fate of

Pilviski where was what the Austrians were most concerned about as they had left behind a garrison at the site from a earlier retreat. The garrison would occasionally try to escape the Russian control, but being since they were surrounded by enemy lines, there was not much that they could accomplish, and on March 22nd, the Austrians at Pilviski eventually surrendered in surrender to Russians.

The spring thaw had begun to take hold which meant more challenges for soldiers in the ground. Although they might be hoping for a resolution to the winter cold and the soft muddy soil that was forming beneath their feet was not suitable for ground combat. It was worse that on April 10, the Russians temporarily stopped the Carpathian campaign to an end. Even with the cessation of fighting, the Austrians were still struggling to recover from the blows that Russians have dealt the country.

With 755,000 deaths, it seemed that it would not be long before Austria-Hungary was knocked out completely of the war. Even though the Austrians were in the midst of defeat, they faced an adamant and fierce enemy within the Germans. However, the Russians faced their fair troubles too. As they were forced to enroll more and more citizens into the military of war, the tensions in a already divided Russian society only grew.

The Russians were quite dissatisfied with their czar for a long time, and as conflict was costing huge sums of blood and money the cracks that were forming in Russian society began to show. Extreme political parties were exploiting these cracks to push their own idealistic visions of what society ought to be. Communist leaders, in particular, gained a growing following and were well-known for their disdain against the czar as well as the Russian the royal family.

Even with their principal adversary in the war Austria-Hungary being in hiding and a close defeat, it wasn't long before the cracks appearing within Russian society would grow into massive fractures. At present it was clear that Russia's Russian army was faithfully carrying up the instructions of their czar. But the day will come when his directives were not heard.

Chapter 7: Allied March On The Ottoman Empire

It was the Ottoman Empire that had more to earn and most to lose in what would happen in World War One. If the Ottomans allies did well and they were successful, it could have enabled the empire's decline to be reclaimed the territory it had lost. This could be an opportunity for the known as the "sick person in Europe" to recover. (This is, of course, isn't how the story was played out in the end, and instead of winning following the loss of the war, the Ottomans fell to the bottom of the barrel.)

However, during World War One, there were instances when it was the Ottomans were able to take the day, proving this long-standing Muslim empire was definitely not a joke in any way. This was evident in The Battle of Gallipoli.

The prelude towards the Battle of Gallipoli stems back to British efforts in February 1915 to push their to cross the Dardanelles. They first heavily bombarded the Turks coastal bases, and then attempted to destroy all mines in the area. On February 25 the military bases were completely destroyed and all mines there were neutralized.

This effort would turn out to be very meaningless when on the 8th of March on March 8th, the "Nursat" (a Turkish minelayer) moved across the channel, laying fresh, brand new mines. The next phase of the assault which was later fought by it was the Royal Marines were sent in to take down additional artillery that was based on land as British naval craft fired on massive guns located within the town of Kephez in the vicinity of Kephez and Kum Kale. After all of these attacks after which it was decided that the British high command determined Turkey to be in good shape to host British troops.

The view was reinforced by the British successfully snuck into an German communication that stated it was clear that Turks were in the process of running out of ammunition. If ever there was a time when Turkey was in the midst of an invasion of its territory then the British decided that it was right now. That's why, on the 18th of March that the Allied fleet launched a coordinated assault on the Dardanelles strait, the narrow one that is the traditional line that separates the region of Turkey that is believed to be part of the Middle East from the smaller northwestern part which makes up the European continent.

The Allies suffered a major hit from the beginning of the war at the time it was the French combat ship, Bouvet which was hit by a mine was torn into the water, leading to deaths of 643 people. While the British tried to defend that waterway against mines over the past few days because of the Turk's redeployment on March 8th however, they were able to miss many. The Brits themselves were the ones who would be next struck by these deadly explosives that were waterborne and The HMS Irresistible and the HMS Inflexible being destroyed.

Following this disaster, another British craft was launched, that of the HMS Ocean was sent to aid the damaged vessels. It was complete disaster. Not long into the rescue mission it was discovered that the HMS Ocean struck a mine and was severely damaged before sinking towards the bottom of ocean. Despite the loss, some of the top brass within the Allied high command believed that if they kept going and fought, they might be able to subdue the Dardanelles to surrender. Some, though, saddened by the losses (and worried about the worsening weather) declared the naval attack off.

It wasn't until April when the Allies attempted a third landing. It was the first Allied military landing in Turkey was carried out on the 25th of April. troops on the ground were brought towards the shore and towed into the beach by steamboats. The group was comprised of consisting of Australian as well as New Zealand troops, which collectively became known as ANZAC.

Initially their landing seemed uncontested. The weapons of Turkey were quiet. However, it was the 19th Turkish Division, led by Lieutenant Colonel Mustafa Kemal - the future leader of an independent Turkey was able to charge into the group with a colossal intensity. Kemal himself would later remember the way his troops acted during the attack and would say, "everybody hurled himself on the enemy in order to kill them and be killed. This was not an ordinary assault. Everyone was determined to win or move forward with the intention of dying."

Even though there was a sense that the Ottoman Empire was declining The Allied powers did not appreciate the fighting spirit that Turks. Turks themselves. Now that the Allies were able to set onto their territory and occupy their territory, the Turks were ready to wipe out those who invaded or die trying. The ANZAC battalions were unable to resist this ferocious attack and were swiftly taken back. However, just in time to be pulled into the ocean they managed to hold on and rally around the bridgehead, which was a tiny part of it.

On April 25, British troops would land at Helles in the southwestern portion of Gallipoli - a peninsula that lies off the northwestern portion of the Turkish mainland. The following day, British troops were able to move forward against the Turks by removing them of the most important locations. The British then continued their advance to Achi Baba in what was later referred to as"the "First Crithia Battle" on the 28th of April. Following this battle, the Turks began a major counterattack at the late in the night. The timing was picked to keep British British off guard and not be shelled by British warships that were parked within the Strait.

The Turks (in huge numbers) were in a position to take on the British regiments. Both sides suffered massive casualties, however the Brits were able to stand their position. The result was an uneasy stalemate, and a fight that went between the two sides, with the one side winning a bit while the other losing some, over the next couple of months. Then, in May the British began to be keen to move the battle again, and so they brought more troops in to relaunch offensives that began on May 6th 1915.

However, under the heavy bombardment of the Turks After a few days it became apparent that they weren't going to be able. It's sad to note that the British made only 600 yards before suffering 6500 casualties within their army. They were able to decide that they'd need to stand firm and stand their ground until reinforcements arrived.

After having bolstered their forces after bolstering their units, after bolstering their troops, the British offensive was launched yet again on the 4th of June 1915. The battle was an actual marathon race through the trenches. the British were able to rise from their fortifications to pour into the field, as artillery and machine gun slashed out. As if a runner jumped over obstacles, they ran across blood-stained and gore-filled trenches that were muddy, trying to gain by a few feet. They continued to push into the Turks defensive lines, as Turks emerged like weasels out of their nests and hurled bombs at the British while they walked over.

A large number of British soldiers were killed in the battle, however some were able to make it to the Turks' main trenches which was a scene of chaos and destruction. The fighting was in the majority of cases involving hand-to-hand combat and bayonets, British battled with the intensity of wild animals while they fought to take control over this Turkish foothold. It soon became evident that they wouldn't be able to further advance.

At this point, a few within the British government wanted to pull the Gallipoli campaign completely However, when the matter was discussed at an assembly on June 7 the young Winston Churchill who strongly advocated that reinforcements be sent to complete the Gallipoli campaign first ahead of turning the complete power of the Allies on the Germans. Churchill was able to convince the committee and at the conclusion of the day, it was agreed that five additional divisions would be sent out to strengthen the troops located in Turkey.

Following the arrival of new recruits, the initial phase of the renewed attack took place on the 6th. It was a literal rerun of the attack conducted during June, an contingent of British soldiers were and sent soaring over the trenches towards those on the Turkish principal lines. However, this time the mission was as a bold detour to intentionally draw the attention of the Turks as a second troop was directed to attack them, as they backed away.

The group that led the first charge was able to predict enough results: they made it across the line in a matter of yards but were repelled by a counterattack and losing thousands of lives. (Instances like this would be a symbol of the complete insanity of trench warfare and in some cases, the entire course of World War One as a total.) And what about the new recruits who were meant to be awe-inspiring for the Turks when they were being diverted by different Allied divisions?

As absurd as it might seem, they got lost on their way. After they left the trenches, they were shot at by the snipers. Then, somewhere in the chaos they made the wrong path and couldn't get back to the battleground. As football players do when they go around in the wrong direction on the field this group of untrained recruits thwarted the heroic efforts of their fellow soldiers by not getting to their intended destination.

When a part of the group finally arrived but they were from being able to do any good. Gallipoli was gone in the early part of January 1916 the entire British as well as Allied forces were pulled out of Turkey with an estimated loss of life of 300,000. The British thought they could easily snuff out the Turks off however this Allied advance through the heart of the Ottoman Empire was evidently a failure.

Chapter 8: The Battle Of Verdun

The Battle of Verdun is one of the most famous combats in the conflict. The battle is known as being the "longest combat" to take place in World War One, this war was fought in the city Verdun, France. It started on February 21, 1916, and wouldn't end until the last day in the calendar year. Most often, the person blamed for this calamity by General Erich von Falkenhayn. German general Erich von Falkenhayn, who was believed to have given an instruction to "bleed the French army into a coma."

The purpose of the German attack in Verdun The goal of the German incursion in Verdun, as you can see, was not to conquer territory, but rather to create the greatest loss of life on the enemy to frighten them to submission. This type of tactic, which involved the use of all-out warfare to overwhelm an adversary is a common practice among Germans through World War One. Outnumbered and surrounded by a variety of nations The Germans tried to pack all their resources into one single blow. With this plan of all-or-nothing in place The German army began their operations in the area of Verdun towards the end of February, which was cold and cold in 1915.

The fighting started in the hills near Verdun at the time that the Germans stationed there launched an ad hoc assault at the French Second Army. The attack began with a torrent of more than 1,220 German guns exploding at the positions of enemy troops in what some called a "symphony in destruction." Slamming into the French with a sledgehammer within the first couple of days, the Germans were able to capture their own Fort Douaumont. French Fort Douaumont. The battle ended as the French brought in more troops to face the threat.

At the time of this writing, Falkenhayn's plan to shake the French with the highest casualty rate was already accomplished, when French reinforcements eased the attack. In early May , the French tried to take back Fort Douaumont, but only was able to take control of some of Fort Douaumont. The situation remained in this unpredictability of the joint German/French occupation until a huge German counterstrike was able to dislodge the French remaining French.

After the Germans gained ground In June, they began to strike at Fort Vaux. They were able to surround Fort Vaux, and entrap the soldiers inside, and then isolating the fort and forcing them to surrender on the 7th of June in 1916. From here, they then seized another French fort--Fort Fleury-devant-Douaumont. The infamous battles between the two sides of World War One would continue the pattern here, since the fort within the following weeks would be divided to those fighting the Germans in addition to the French for a total of 16 times!

The moment this small parcel of land was taken and then reclaimed by competing hands, it is easy to imagine the German screaming in victory, "Wunderbar! This is my!" only for a Frenchmen just a few seconds afterward to shout "Non! It's a me!" The situation had been so absurd that the main architect of Verdun General Falkenhayn was actually dismissed from his position. His aim of inflicting massive deaths on the French was now an unsettling exchange with both the French along with Germans Germans over positions of minimal strategic significance.

It wasn't until the 18th of August that the Germans were able to take over Fort Vaux fortification. Fort Vaux fortification for good. While this conflict continued to rage in a plethora of French forts, many lives were lost both sides. It was the Battle of Verdun didn't begin to end until November, 1916 in the event that the French captured Fort Vaux. The French made one last frenzied assault on December 15th just before they were defeated. Battle of Verdun ended.

The reason that the battle at Verdun was halted was due to an important juncture of battle, Germany was forced to assign forces to its Eastern Front to fend off the Russians. The final battle resulted in the loss of 377,321 French and 377,321 German lives. The objective was to destroy the French however, just about the same number of German life was lost in the bloody, gruesome deadlock that Verdun became.

It was so awful the fact that, during World War Two, when the Germans were in a tense struggle against the Russians in Stalingrad, Hitler specifically invoked this conflict that he had experienced during World War One, telling his troops that the Germans did not "want to see another Verdun." Verdun was the Battle of Verdun had come to represent more than any other incident in World War One, the unrelenting sands of the trenches. People had laid their lives in the thousands in order to move just a few feet. Verdun will always be an ominous warning in the direction of unjust destruction and war.

Chapter 9: The Great Russian Rebound

The initial days of 1916 saw the Russian army appearing almost smug during the initial months that were largely unoccupied on the Russian frontlines. The Russian army's war machine did not advance until March 18th in 1916. The offensive was comprised of eight separate battles that were executed from mid-March until April 14th. These assaults were able to penetrate into the German front and push the Russians ahead for nearly one mile.

The Russians continued to grind to a standstill as they consolidated their successes and assessed their situation. In the midst of this latest pause in battle the Russian top command determined that any additional action taken in the moment would be too costly, given that the German forces were superior in artillery, and the Russians were struggling to not be able to replenish their ammunition.

However, the Germans did regroup after this time and were soon at it again. On the 28th of April they swarmed across the Russian front, and then sank into Russian territory for about three miles. As was typical during this conflict in the war, the Russians just gathered their troops, and then pushed their Germans away, and Russian troops returning almost the exact spot they had been. However, one major difference between Germans as well as the Russians there was that Russia was able to use a virtually infinite amount of troops.

In reality, the German army was more restricted in its reserve troops. Particularly after the bloody mishap that was Verdun in the Western Front, the chance to get German reinforcement in the East from the west became very slim. Thus, the Germans were ahead in terms of military equipment and tools but Russia retained its lead in terms of the sheer amount of troops put together.

However, despite its huge workforce, the nation's workers were in the process of going to a strike that would last for a long time. While the communist idealism could have come from an influential German known as Karl Marx, it was in Russia where his ideas would eventually be able to take root when those who were known as "Bolsheviks" began organizing strikes across Russia and encouraging general unrest. One of the men who would later become the first leader of the communist party in Russia, Vladimir Lenin, was also at work in the midst of this, blasting out propaganda literature in which he urged ordinary people around the globe to revolt against their "capitalist bosses."

For Russia Of course it was a call for peasant soldiers to rebel and oppose fighting to support Russian Czar Nicholas. Communist revolutionaries such as Lenin were actively looking to inflame divisions, creating an acrimony between the masses of the poor and their elitist and privileged overseers. In a time where Russia was in need of forming united to defend itself against German military aggressions, this unstable political system would turn out to be a disaster. As supplies dwindled on both the frontline as well as in Russian supermarkets the disaster recipe was in place, and within a short time the widespread defection and insurrection within the ranks would become normal.

However, during 1917, in the cohesion was still in place for a bigger offensive. It was referred to as the "Brusilov Offensive" the major battle was comprised of Russian divisions fighting Austro-Hungarian troops within the Galicia region. Galicia. The Russians could achieve a numerical advantage by having their 200,000 troops competing against 150,000 Austrian troops. This meant that they Russian Eighth Army was able to slash through the gathered Austrians and advance towards Lutsk which was where the Russians tried to increase their gains.

The most important aspect to the Allied efforts to win the war the successful attack resulted in the redirection of German forces from West back towards in the Eastern Front, because as shortly as Germany became aware of how badly their Austrian counterparts were and immediately dispatched four entire battalions to fight the Russians. In doing so, they substantially weakened their stance in Verdun and the Western Front - most especially Verdun and allowed the French to mount a massive and extremely successful counterattack on the 23rd of June. In a war with endless reversals of fortune the Russian attack could have a lot of consequences for the entire Allied efforts to win the war.

Chapter 10:, America Is A Participant In Into War For The Allies

Americans felt a bit disengaged from the developments taking place in Europe and the majority of them would prefer to let the conflict than become involved. The non-interventionist and isolationist spirit was so strong so that the president Woodrow Wilson ran his 1916 election campaign with the catchy phrase, "he kept us out of the war." The caption of the campaign was a reference to the steps undertaken by Wilson to prevent American involvement in the earlier point in the war.

Following when the British ship Lusitania was destroyed by the German submarine which killed 128 Americans aboard despite the saber-rattling of a few, Wilson had allowed cooler heads to prevail. Instead of launching a the warfront, Wilson had successfully talked off the Germans and negotiated a promise from them not to strike passenger ships in the near future. Wilson tried to present his self as an engineer for peace instead of a warmonger However, shortly after his reelection and his victory, war would be on the horizon in the same way.

It wasn't too long after the second inauguration in the month of January 1917 that the Germans were able to revert to their pledge and began to engage in unlimited submarine warfare. The German submarine fleet was now over 150, and they now determined to deploy them whenever and wherever. Through sinking merchant ships, they sought to destroy vital shipment of ammunition as well as other war materials.

In addition to the reports of Germans threat to commercial vessels time, Britain would uncover a surprise of a completely different order. British agents had discovered an email sent by German foreign minister to officials in Mexico. German Foreign Minister to Mexican officials Mexico asking the Mexican government to join forces with Germany and saying that if they did so, Germany will assist Mexico to regain its former territory that comprised New Mexico, Texas, and Arizona.

President Wilson was obviously shocked by the developments. Apparently not sure of his next move so he decided to make public information from the fraudulent message to the media and let the public's opinion determine his choices for him. Realizing that the public was ready to be killed, Wilson then began to shift his tone instead of abstaining from the war with all his might the president began to speak of having to have a "war that would end all wars."

In this belief, he believed that the moment was right to fight an impartial war in order to cleanse the world of militarism that is rampant. Wilson was of the opinion that, if one single police act could be accomplished - resolving injustices on a massive scale - peace in the world could be achieved. Being aware of the widespread support for his idea and that he had the support of his fellow Americans, President Wilson was able to declare the war against Germany on April 6 in 1917. The pace of events accelerated from there. Around 2.8 million Americans were recruited into the army. And by 1918 , it was estimated that 10,000 soldiers were deployed into the Western Front every single day.

In interestingly, it was in order to support the conscription effort to aid in the conscription efforts that American citizenship was initially granted to residents of that U.S. territories in Puerto Rico.

Germany in turn was shocked that their intractable enemies were now receiving new soldiers from America. They intensified efforts to oust from the British and French prior to the Americans came to the scene.

After the declaration of war Patriotism in America increased to the highest levels. However, there was a lot of discrimination against American citizens from Germany. It was remarkable that the American people could mobilise themselves to fight Germany however, the negative of this enthusiasm was that it triggered a bias and distrust of anyone and everything German.

In the days when Germany was the aggressor and everyone who had German family ties was forced to dissociate themselves from their ancestral roots. For those Americans who were washed up on American shores earlier the newer immigrants with their thick accents and distinct German manners would have to face some of the most sexist prejudices of their lives.

No matter what sentiment in the matter, America was about to enter World War One. The first group of 14000 U.S. troops would arrive in France on June 26, 1914. However, these troops weren't fully prepared for battle. They would first need to train, drill and equip themselves with the appropriate equipment to fight in the trenches.

The German top command was concerned regarding their concerns about the American presence, however certain people tried to minimize the importance of the troop increase particularly due to the brutality in the German U-Boat battle. The joke was that the Americans were expected to arrive "naked" as the bulk of their provisions were dumped in the ocean in the days prior to when they arrived. This could have been a nice joke to tell to the German troops however they would discover how untrue they actually were. When the Americans were inducted, given their weapons and set free on the battlefield, the Germans wouldn't be laughing any longer.

Chapter 11: Italy Under Siege

Italy was a baffling factor during World War One. Through the course of the war it was unclear for certain of which side Italy was on or how long it would be as a loyal partner. There were many aspects that Italy was a recently unification nation as Germany has a lot similarity to the Germans with regard to the general goals for nation building. However, while the Italians were able to have a lot in the same way as the Germans however, they faced huge differences with Germany's primary allies, Austria-Hungary.

Italy was at war with its neighbor Austria-Hungary from the time Italy became a sovereign and independent country from Austria-Hungary in 1870. There were territorial disputes between the two were able to argue over the decades that were to follow (especially in the dispute over the areas in Trieste as well as Trentino) and, by the period of World War One, Italy considered it an ideal chance to support Austria-Hungary's enemies to settle the scores.

Many ways the decision of Italy of joining the Allies was a gamble in the same way as it was an act of revenge. When it became evident that Italy did not want to be a part of the Germans The Allies particularly, the British began to aggressively seek out Italy to be a potential partner during the war. This eventually resulted in an agreement known as the Treaty of London on April 26th, 1915, which Italy decided to declare war on central powers so long as certain gains in territorial territory from Austria-Hungary were given to it, like the strategic port at Trieste.

After the agreement was signed, Italy went ahead and declared war on Austria-Hungary on the 23rd of May, 1915. The Italians quickly established the known as Trent, Trentino, and Alpine fronts, which were located just below the Isonzo River. It was from this area that they decided to take the fight against the Austrians. The Italians were armed with around 850,000 during the fight. Ten years before dictator Benito Mussolini was to establish his fascist regime (Benito was actually an ordinary soldier at the period) the Italian government was led by the Italian Emperor Victor Emanuel. In his aegis were strong Italian generals, like general Luigi Cadorna.

The primary issue Italy confronted during World War One was similar to the one that afflicted the Russians and Russians, which was that they were frequently inadequately equipped. But, just following the announcement was signed in accordance with their words they Italians made their way towards the Isonzo and pushed the Austrians further away. The Italians were able to advance towards the east of Isonzo before they came to the ground. From the beginning they Italians were adamant and a determination to overwhelm their adversaries. It's fascinating to consider that as brave as the Italians were in World War One, much of this enthusiasm would become severely lacking during World War Two.

In any case at the time of the First World War the Italians appeared to be ready for business. However even with their enthusiasm, their determination would be stopped during the "First Battle of Isonzo," on June 23rd 1915. In this battle, the Italians could make only very small advances on the field prior to either being forced back or fighting to a deadlock. In the overall nature of trench-to-troop fighting during World War One, the Italians as well as the Austrians were soon caught trapped in a bloody and intractable impasse.

There were 9 Battles of Isonzo, in which the same scenario would occur. In this tale of two sides of fortunes, it was the Fifth Battle of Isonzo, on the 11th March 1916 which the Austrians were able to gain the upper hand and were able to push their Italians back. Through a fierce artillery bombardment and a ruthless drive through the mountains before moving on to the plains of the coast. In this area, they were able to break communication with Italian communications lines, stopping updates from reaching Italian commanders.

It was the Austrians advanced until the almost reached to the Po River in Northern Italy's coastal plains. What did not stay in the Austrian side was that Russia was also delivering severe hits to Austria-Hungary in the Eastern Front, and as consequently they have been forced to slow down their advancement towards Italy to divert more troops towards the east. When this latest round was coming to an end in the end, the Italians suffered losses of 147,000 as the Austrians were able to lose 81,000 of their soldiers in the battle.

It was quiet in the Italian front until the 6th of August 1916, which saw the conclusion of the Sixth Battle of Isonzo, where the Italians were again not able to achieve any gains. They seized, most notably, their town Gorizia. In Gorizia, the Austrians battled the Italians in open areas in fierce, close-quartered combat that could be used as as guns.

Italy had at that time only declared war against Austria-Hungary. However, it made the decision during the raging war to declare war against Austria's partner Germany on August 28 in 1916.

The Italians were able to defeat those Austrians at Gorizia but, because of the number of casualties Italian troops suffered the battle could be considered to be an Pyrrhic victory, at the very least. From the moment they got until Isonzo's Ninth Battle of Isonzo, the Italians could not hope to advance further and the death toll of the bloody battle increased.

Following this, the Italians discovered themselves either battling the Austrians or under attack from the Austrians. We could go through the progresses and retreats but reliving what transpired during this constant reversal of fortunes could be so redundant to be almost absurd. The only thing that changed this mess came when Russian front fell in the east, allowing the Austrians to focus all their efforts on their Italian rivals.

Chapter 12: The Great Russian Collapse

The beginning of the year was not a good one for Russians and, as early as in January of 1917, it appeared that the whole Russian regime appeared to be in danger of falling. Protests against the Czar was at its peak as resources at home as well as in the Russian front were at their lowest. There was no one who believed that the war was over but, more crucially, nobody believed in the direction that was Czar Nicholas Alexandrovich Romanov any longer.

The entire sentiment would get to the forefront in the known as "February Revolution" that was declared to bring off the Russian czar to end his reign. When dissent and protest started to rise on the streets in St. Petersburg, on March 11, the czar made a decision to send in troops to restore some sense of order. But the crowd was in a state of chaos and disorder and, despite repeated orders that they would not stand down.

When the crowd seemed to be close to becoming beyond control, police were convinced that they were forced to open fire on the demonstrators. The sight of blood spilled was only a way to inspire the protesters. Instead of stopping them the bloodshed only encouraged them to be even more radical. The soldiers charged with reining the protesters started to feel guilty for not embracing their fellow citizens which led many to abandon their superiors and join the other protesters instead.

When his own army departed from him, the czar was left with the option of resigning. After his resignation, the czar was able to agree that a temporary government be put in place until the next leader was appointed. The czar's thoughts were that there was no way he would quit the monarchy. Even if he didn't become the monarch at the moment the czar had planned to replace Michael as his brother Michael when the smoke gone away. However, this was never to happen.

After a couple of months of the provisories deliberations over what type of government to be established the next time, Russia was subject to an unpopular communist coup. The coup was dubbed"the "October Revolution" the Marxist takeover was largely a result of the communist ideologue Vladimir Lenin. The communists were able to attract an impressive number of troops behind their cause, and thanks to this support, they were able to seize crucial power stations as well as post offices, banks depots for trains and other infrastructures that were important. This was the first step to Lenin and his revolutionaries to take over the Winter Palace, where the interim government had been established and to install the communist government to replace it.

What about the war which raged across the Eastern Front? Lenin effectively declared war over. The communists refused to engage in the war of the czar and would as quickly put it aside completely. But in the near future, it was the German military, encouraged through their experience with Russian turmoil, was going to give them with no choice in the situation.

To confront the reality of war, Lenin did manage to negotiate a cease-fire for a short period on the 15th of December, 1917 but it was only an insignificant interlude. In addition to fearing the Germans, Lenin also had to deal with issues in Ukraine as well as the tense civil war the Russian leader would have to face in Russia at large, since factions that were unwilling to accept the outcomes that came from October Revolution October Revolution would continue to be a source of contention for the communists' ear for the period of three years to come.

Meanwhile, communists were faced with a significant task to do: reforming the Russian army from one of the imperial arms of the Czar to becoming a communist-run force that would become known by the name of "Red Army." One benefit that the newly retooled army enjoyed was that the bitter resentment against the Russian royal family was completely eliminated. In actual fact it was they were the Russian royal family was eliminated as Nicholas and his wife and their children were killed by the Bolsheviks.

This horrific act allowed the Russian military to shift into an entirely new revolutionary guard. The superficial change was not enough to take on an increasingly powerful German military that was poised to slam through the front doors of Russia. By March of that year, the Germans were in fact only 85 miles away from St. Petersburg - a extremely real reason for the new communist government to be worried.

Lenin realized that it was impossible for his troubled Russia would be able to stand this war, so the Russian leader sought a way to get out. Although he knew that the terms were severe, he requested an agreement to end the war to the Germans. This was made possible on the 3rd of March 1918 in the Treaty of Brest-Litovsk. The treaty's terms specified that the newly formed "Soviet Union" of Russia will renounce any previous objectives and alliances of the previous Imperial Russia.

But this isn't all. It was also the case that Russians were also obliged to surrender a massive quantity of the territory that been part of the former Russian Empire. The entire Baltic states, which were earlier territories of Russia were required to be handed over to Germany and the territory of the Caucuses was to be transferred to Germany's partner , the Ottoman Empire, while Ukraine was, in turn, to be given independence.

It was a painful humiliation however, should it be enough to make the communist Russians out of a conflict they didn't want to be fighting at all They were prepared to accept the conditions. It was for them just a temporary setback. In addition, Lenin and his cohorts were of the opinion that what they heard from the Germans gave them would not have any impact in the long term because they believed that their idea about "world communism" would spread to other regions of Europe quickly, rendering any agreement they made non-constitutional and unenforceable.

In the coming months, Lenin would only be confirmed partially in his claim. Germany was ultimately defeated in the war and all obligations Russia agreed to within the Treaty of Brest-Litovsk would indeed be deemed obsolete. However, Lenin's idea of world communism did not be as popular as he had hoped it would. The Germans were able to avoid becoming an communist state following the war. By removing the Marxists the fascists would be at Germany's doorstep, instead.

Chapter 13: The Turkish Battle Of Armageddon

Popular legend and religious tradition have frequently spoken of an epic battle that would take place at the end of the time, also known as Armageddon however, many are unaware that Armageddon is actually a location and that the battle was actually in some sense already fought by the British as well as The Ottoman Turks in the trenches of World War One. There's a region in Palestine it is true that was initially called Tel Meggido. The Greeks who call it Armageddon.

In earlier times, Meggido was used as a garbage dump for burning waste. when it was the scene of a significant conflict which resulted in the loss of many lives in the area and the corpses were frequently burned in Meggido as well. This is the place where the myth of the apocalypse surrounding Meggido's desert region comes from. When the British were fighting those Ottoman Turks there, the images were not lost on all the Allied troops.

The prelude to Armageddon started with the known as "First Battle of Gaza" which took place in the region that lies between Egypt as well as Palestine. In this area, the 53rd and54th divisions attempted to block Turkish positions within the region using an iconic pincer movement however, they were driven back by fierce fighting. In addition was that it was clear that the Turks had fortified the small area of land so firmly (with trenches strewn with cactus, no more) the area was likely to be a very difficult task. However, the Brits persevered and were able to defeat the trenches in the initial line with the help of several Turkish prisoners in the process.

When it came to the Second Battle of Gaza, which was fought on April 19th 1917, the battle didn't go so well. The cactus-lined trenches were more formidable, with guns poking through the tough hedges. Just one look at these fortifications and an common soldier was awestruck.

Looking to achieve using machines what was incredibly difficult to accomplish with bone and flesh In order to accomplish what would be incredibly difficult with bone and flesh, the British confiscated a few from their Mark I tanks - some of the first to take on action in battle. They believed that the massive tanks could glide right over the fortifications and save their infantrymen from being killed by the buzz saws of Cacti and machine guns. However, those tanks in World War One were far different from the tanks of World War Two.

They were extremely inefficient, crawling across the battlefield. They were extremely hot inside, making it difficult for tankers to remain inside their tanks for very long. Two factors made the transportation of these giants to the deserts in the Middle East quite impractical. As they moved they were also subject to failures, which caused additional issues. Tanks would often not reach the trenches , before or breaking down by themselves or being crushed into scrap by repeatedly direct strikes by Turkish large artillery.

The loss of military equipment was a major embarrassment for those in the British high command. seeking to redress the debacle, they dismissed the officer in charge of his position. His replacement was an ex-commanding officer of the Western Front, General Sir Edmund Allenby. Allenby after arriving at his spot, instantly altered his tactics. Instead of attempting to take over the main fortifications of Gaza and the surrounding areas, he directed his troops' attention to taking the nearby Beersheba in a region in which the defenses weren't much more formidable.

The Third Battle of Gaza ensued and, after just a few days fighting and fighting, the British won the battle by breaking through the Turkish lines in Beersheba. Once they had gotten through the wall the British were able to swiftly route towards Jerusalem with the British arriving at their gates to the old city in December of 1917. Allenby determined to enter the city on foot to avoid the fury of being seen as an emperor and gain the city almost without opposition.

In Meggido in the meantime the battle was getting ready to begin. Both sides would take their heels in the landscape, and would spend the next months working towards a massive clash. After a series of stops and starts during the battle It was during the early early morning hours of September 19th 1918 that Allenby with 35,000 men of infantry force and a 9000-man cavalry and a 9000-man cavalry - swarmed into the field of Armageddon.

From the very beginning, the war seemed more like an end-of-the world the Turks as it was for the British because it was the Turkish battle lines were destroyed. In the end, Turkey suffered irreparable injury. On the 30th of October, Turkey was knocked out of the war totally, as well as the Ottoman Empire that held supremacy across this region of Middle East for centuries had been dissolved. As far as it was the British as well as those involved in the Allied War effort were concerned at most for the time being there was no doubt that the Battle of Armageddon had been won.

Chapter 14: Germany Loses The War

Despite their successes over their Eastern Front, with their allies, the Ottoman Empire eliminated from fighting, chances that Germany winning the war became increasingly slim. The Allies who were free of conflicts with North Africa and the Middle East and North Africa they could now spend significant resources to fight the German danger in Europe. However the armistice Germany recently signed with Russia has ended their war in the Eastern Front, giving the Germans an opportunity to try to re-energize their positions on their Western trenches.

However, by 1918 it was clear that it was clear that the German high command was faced with something new to worry about, the mobilization and deployment of a group of new-faced soldiers in America. United States of America. The fear of being overwhelmed who had the German high command moving into a frenetic new period of warfare. They believed that with one final frenzied rush they could eliminate their Allies ahead of time before Americans were able to arrive.

It was this desire for action that caused the German offensive into Allied territories on the Somme River in the Western Front on the 21st of March, 1918. German soldiers fought British troops. British Fifth Army. The Germans began their attack according to their usual tactics, around 4 a.m. and commenced the assault with a ferocious bombardment of artillery. A phrase like "the barrage was fierce" is commonplace during these instances of war, but as per those present this particular incident may have been more intense than other.

As per the statement of Lt. Herbert Sulzbach of the 63rd Field Artillery, battle began with "thousands as well as thousands mortars and gun barrels and mortars, a barrage that sounded like the world is closing in." If you witnessed the devastation, down in the trenches under the constant blasts of explosives it certainly appear as if the earth was poised to fall on the verge of the brink of collapse.

Following the initial trenches and trenches, they Royal Artillery were the next to be confronted by the German assault with many gas bombs mixed by regular shells of artillery fired towards them. In the case of gas thrown at them there three distinct phases of the chemical war. The Germans had achieved the perfect chemical warfare and as absurd as it might sound, even took the initiative to color-code them in accordance with the effects.

There were blue and green canisters, as well as yellow canisters. The blue canisters contained gas that, while not lethal in nature, could cause anyone who smelt of it to gag, cough and throw up rapidly. The Germans were aware that when the gas was used in large quantities and a portion of it was released, it could eventually get into gas masks worn by the enemy and result in them vomiting. Naturally, the first reaction of someone who vomits in their gas mask is to take off their gas mask in order to throw up.

That's exactly what was exactly what the Germans wanted to accomplish. When the enemy was given enough time to take off their masks, and then lie down in their trenches and throw up in their trenches, the Germans would then unleash the green canisters that contained Phosphene gas, that was certainly lethal. Then, it was followed by a blast of mustard gas so deadly that it was guaranteed to kill regardless of whether other strategies did not work. As these obscene exercises show to, the German military was long gone from any mercy or restraint in pursuit of defeating their adversaries.

It was during the midst this terrible chaotic situation that Germans could break into the "Forward Zone" of the British trenches. This was the first major barrier in Allied defence to be broken. Then attack, the German infantry fought against an area known as the "Battle Zone" which consisted of the second stage of fortifications. The Germans were positioned to the center of the Fifth Army.

It was a long day of brutal and relentless combat, and the following day would not be any more different. With barely enough time to breathe and rest, they Germans (under the shadow of thick fog) began a new attack the next day, the 22nd of March and pushed the British back up to Crozat Canal in their ferocious assault. While the British fled to safety to escape, they encountered a brand new danger: German airplanes! While airplanes played a less important role during World War One, mostly used for reconnaissance, and sometimes dogfights, in some air battles, airplanes participated.

This was also the case during the particular siege, German pilots took off low just over the trenches and fired at the fleeing British using their machine guns. The result was chaos when it was reported that the German Aces flew around, picking off the poor British one at a time. Some British veterans would later say that planes flew so low and so close they pulled out their revolvers on the go to shoot at them. However, the shots the British fired with their guns did not have any effect on the daring pilots.

The Germans clearly gave the battle everything they had and under the constant assault they were able to break through the British lines on the Somme river, crossing it on the 24th of March. When when the Germans traversed the Somme and the British were forced further west.

All this aggression was a huge cost to the Germans as the farther west they moved and the further they pushed their communications and ammunition lines were. When their German army became less organized and disoriented and confused, the

British took reserve troops in to strike a brutal hit. On the 26th of March, replenished British forces literally took from"the "big guns" and set up massive pieces of artillery across the trenches. They began to pound German groups of soldiers one after the other. They were able of destroying the German infantry with such ease that one British officer said it was akin to "target training on the Salisbury Plain"!

In the meantime, massive amounts of additional Allied troops returning from completed combats within the Middle East began to converge on the Western Front, making the location of the Germans extremely dangerous. The Germans who were severely wounded and weakened, were forced to take refuge in the trenches. For time only a matter of to heal their wounds. They didn't come out until the 4th of April and that was when the German infantry exploded and again advancing towards the town of Villers Brettonneux, in the area of Amiens.

However, a few of those reinforcements which included an elite bunch comprised of Australian infantrymen, were able to make short task of the Germans eventually putting the brakes on their march. As the latest phase of battles was over in the end, the Germans had gained several miles of sand and mud across the Western Front at the cost of 239,000 of their own lives. After the bloodshed and efforts the Germans' efforts to reverse the tide been unsuccessful.

However however, it was clear that the German high command did not intend to quit but they changed their tactics. They were now planning an attempt to snare those British forces in Flanders, the French region of Flanders which is located within Northern France. In Flanders, they wanted to encircle, isolate and eliminate a significant part of the British military. It was also their intention to destroy the British lines and capture the important train depot at Hazebrouk that would assist in their eventual takeover of the ports that were vital to Dunkirk and Calais along Calais, which lie on the French coast.

Despite this new place however, the Germans adhered to their traditional plan of action when it came down to battle tactics in unleashing their artillery at Brits Brits during the hours of April 9th, and then bringing troops to the ground a couple of hours later.

Initially it appeared that the Germans performed admirably with their offensive and were able to breach the first line of British defenses in the area. In this battle during the battle, the Germans had advanced approximately five and a quarter miles and had taken about 100 pieces of enemy heavy artillery.

Even though they'd reached five miles of depth but they had not been able to break the British line of defense completely. The Germans continued to push but on the 10th of April, they were in danger of getting close to the depot for trains. In the midst of waiting for their French allies to show up with reinforcements and reinforcements, the British were ready to take the final stand. The prospects were extremely negative, but they Brits had a determination to fight. Before the second phase of the war started on April 11, British Commander-in-Chief, Field Marshal Sir Douglas Haig, tried to inspire his troops with the significance of the time where they were put in.

He told them "Many people are exhausted. For those who are tired, I'd say that victory will go to the team that holds out for the longest time. This French force is moving swiftly and with great force with our full support. There is only one option for us to take but to take on the French army. Each position has to be held until the end of time man. There can not be any retirement. With our backs against the wall and with faith in the rightness of our cause, each of us must continue to fight until the end. Our safety, our families as well as the safety of humanity alike rest on the character of each of us in this crucial moment."

When they heard these words The British soldiers retreated to their positions while the Germans hit them again on the 17th of April 1918. However, like always the British kept their position and defeated the assault. The Germans eager to make a gain, began to target nearby French units stationed at Mount Kemmel, instead. After launching an attack on at the French they were capable of capturing their infantry, however, they were unable to take out the French heavy guns that were in the distance soon started to cause them to regret the move as the heavy shells began batter the Germans to a halt.

The war entered an unsettling new phase for tired combatants who lived in trenches when, on April 24 the first battle ever between two armies of tanks from the enemy began at the Somme. As if everything was planned in some way and planned, both the Germans as well as the British both brought three variants of the massive metal beast into the battlefield simultaneously. All the combat-worn soldiers could be amazed and watch as the Germans gigantic A7V tanks fought the British Mark IV tanks.

It was truly an amazing sight to behold. According to one eyewitness British Lieutenant Frank Mitchell, "Suddenly, out of the ground about 10 feet away an infantryman arose with his rifle and began to scream. We were stopped. He rushed forward and yelled out through the flap, "Look out! Jerry tanks are around!" (Jerry used to be a negative name that the British used to refer to"the Germans.) When the tanks were seen and the Mark IVs were moved forward to fight them. A Mark IV was hit by Germans with armor-piercing rounds and was forced to retreat.

Another Mark IV then came forward and was able to take an immediate strike on the leading German tank. The tank stopped, as if stunned while it fired off another round. British tank fired another round, this time, bringing the tank to a total stop. The Mark IV hit the German tank three times and the blast smashed the tank over. Its German tank crew were seen escaping from the vehicle, and taking off for the hills. This apparently was enough for the two other German tanks to make a run for it, so they decided to withdraw and take the weapons that were not tested of their tanks back to the security of the defensive lines.

It was the Germans' subsequent major attack was on May 27 the 27th of May, 1918. Going back to their normal routine and tactics, the Germans launched their attack in the early hours of the morning with infantry and artillery. The British were under attack in this attack which meant that they Germans had the chance to push forward again, moving approximately 35 miles in British territory. However, as was the regular pattern throughout the conflict, when French reinforcements arrived and the Germans were forced back again.

And not only that, at this point, the Americans were already at their way and appeared prepared to fight the Germans. If the words on the wall was not there prior to this, the German top command was aware in certainty that the war was lost. By the beginning of August, all gains made from the 27th of May had been lost. In late August it was clear that the Germans were increasingly in the defensive, had been driven towards an area known as the Monchy le Preux line.

Then, on the 12th of September the young doughboys - - the Americans took on the leading position in their first offensive. Although the other Allies used to make fun of the Americans being sluggish and untrained (hence the name doughboys) in this battle , they really proved their strength. The Americans ran out into the St. Mihiel salient with guns in the air, while the French Artillery provided them with a constant support barrages.

In the end, Germans were forced to retreat in complete retreat. They tried to retaliate but this massive American offensive ended their chances. The momentum would stay shared by the Allies throughout the war. In a state of insurmountable resistance and unable to withstand any longer, the Germans accepted defeat and declare their surrender on the 11th of November in 1918. With a price tag of more than 37 million deaths and a war that was not able to be over, World War One, was over.

Chapter 15: Europe And The World In 1914

At the beginning of the 20th century, Europe was the main political centre of the globe. It was the United States, though growing in influence and strength but was not the global player that it is today. The most powerful countries that were referred to as"the Great Powers, were Austria - Hungary, France, Germany, Great Britain and Russia.

Austria and Hungary was not a nation , but two distinct entities: it was the Austrian Empire and the kingdom of Hungary which were joined under Emperor Franz-Joseph I of the ancient House of Hapsburg. The two countries weren't united as a whole. They were not united. Austrian Empire was comprised of Germans who ruled over Czechs, Poles, Italians as well as other minorities of ethnicity. The Kingdom of Hungary the ethnic Hungarians were the rulers over Romanians, Serbs, Croats, Ruthenians and other Slavs. This monarchy of Austro Hungary was unstable structure at a time where every ethnic group was looking to define its individual identity. The main goal that people of both the German as well as Hungarian dominant population was to maintain the monarchy and dominated by

Germans within Austria in Austria and by those of the Magyars within Hungary. This meant squeezing the local Slav people.

France also known as France, or the French Third Republic was unique among the European nations due to the fact that the country was not a state. There were only two republics: Switzerland and the small nation that was San Marino in the Italian peninsula. France was the ruler of a large overseas empire that included Morocco, Algeria and Tunisia in Africa, Indochina (now Vietnam) in Asia and French Suriname in South America. France was still reeling from the defeat it suffered in the hands of the Germans during the Franco-Prussian War 1870 - 1871. The German campaign was executed efficiently, in addition, the German Army was equipped with the advantage of technology. Germany gained the Alsace-Lorraine Province. The French were furious and the Alsace-Lorraine province was re-invaded. They believed that their country was recovering from the events of 1871 and that their army was capable of catching Germany. In 1914, the President of France was Raymond Poincare.

The German Empire was an extremely new nation. Germany was an amalgamation of distinct kingdoms, principalities and dukedoms before they were joined through Prussia at the time of 1871. The the kings of Prussia - - the House of Hohenzollernwere made emperors or Kaisers of Germany. The Chancellor Otto Von Bismark had been the architect of the greatness of Prussia and was an accomplished diplomat and politician. In 1914 , the emperor had been Vilhelm II, a volatile person who longed for German glory and was wary of the prospect of diplomatic isolation. Bismark and Wilhelm clashed. Bismark quit and Germany was unable to maintain the stability it required.

The Empire was home to a federal legislature called the Reichstag. In reality, Germany was run by Prussia and its monarchs. Germany had a tiny colonial empire that was not nearly as big as the ones in France or Great Britain. The main strength that was the strength of Germany in the army. Prussia had a strong militaristic culture and its troops were disciplined, modern, and equipped with top technology available. The power of its military was bolstered by an technological industrial economy.

Great Britain possessed the largest empire the world has witnessed which extended from Canada all the way to New Zealand. It was home to the massive subcontinent of India which was regarded as the crown jewel of the British Crown. The wealth of Britain, which was based on the power of its navy, the biggest as well as the most formidable in all of history is the envy of other powerful nations. George V, the grandfather of Elizabeth II, was not just the King of Great Britain, but Emperor of India. The British royals were connected to noble families from Germany. In fact, they came to the rulers from Hanover which was located in the northern part of Germany and George's great-grandfather Albert, who was Queen Victoria's husband and father of his children, gave his family's name, Saxe-Coburg Gotha, to the British royal family. In 1917, the royal name became Windsor to ease German sentiment. A majority of European royalty were linked through marriage or blood with Queen Victoria. Tsar Nicholas II, George V and Vilhelm II were cousins. In the midst of war, the citizens of Europe desperately hoped that familial ties of the grand royal houses would be able to save them. In 1914 , the Prime

Minister for Britain was Herbert Asquith. His replacement was David Lloyd George in 1915.

Russia was a huge nation, stretching across Poland to the west up to Bering Strait, which lies to the east. The majority of the people in that Russian Empire comprised Russian but it also contained Poles, Finns, Lithuanians, Estonians, Turks, Mongols, Georgians and many other ethnic groups. In contrast to Great Britain and France it was an autocracy, and was governed by the wishes of the Tsar or Emperor of Russia. In the House of Romanoff was the ruling family in Russia for more than 300 years. The current representative on the throne is Nicholas II, an ineffectual man who was never one who wanted to be a tsar. In spite of its size, Russia was unpopular politically and socially. nation. It was not until recently that serfdom was removed. It wasn't industrialized in the same way as the major powers of the past were, and most of its citizens was peasants. It was not a legislature. The emperors believed in being chosen by God and had absolute monarchs in power, with the support of the state-approved Russian Orthodox Church.

In 1905, a war of attrition with Japan caused an uprising. People wanted social reforms as well as an constitution. Nicholas II was in agreement with the constitution and created the parliament, or Duma which was a complete disaster to the Romanoffs was avoided. But absolute power was still at the discretion of the emperor, who was required to approve any laws and disband the Duma at his discretion. Thus, in 1914, there was a great deal of unrest across the empire.

It was said that the Russian army was one of the largest in Europe however, it was lacking the resources to sustain and equip the troops. This could have disastrous consequences and ultimately result in the demise of the Romanoff family.

Alongside being part of the Great Powers, two other organizations are worth mentioning. Italy as well as Germany was a fairly new nation. It was made up of many independent nations that included Rome as well as central Italy that had been controlled for about a 1000 years and more under the Pope who was in charge of the Catholic Church. It was the House of Savoy is ruled by the kings of Sardinia and Sardinia, slowly unified the

Italian peninsula in about the halfway point of 19th century. In 1871, Sardinian forces defeated Rome and declared Rome the capital city in the kingdom of Italy. The Prussians helped to establish their new Italy in the face of their old foes, France and Austria. The taking of Rome caused an issue for the newly-established country. The popes refused to recognize the conquer of Rome or the Kingdom of Italy. They retreated towards the Vatican Palace, proclaiming themselves as prisoners. The situation became the focus of the Roman Question which dominated Italian politics until it was resolved in 1929 in which it was the time that the Vatican City State was recognized. The reigning monarch of Italy is Victor Emmanuel III.

Another state that merits some consideration is the Ottoman Empire which was centered around the region we know as Turkey. The Islamic empire, led by the sultans from the House of Osman (Ottoman) and over the whole Balkan Peninsula. In the 19th century, the people of the Balkans comprising Greece, Bulgaria, Romania, Serbia and Montenegro - declared their independence and drove Ottomans back. It was the Great Powers often supported the revolts. Russia particularly wanted to increase its influence in the Balkans and ultimately, the goal of gaining control over Constantinople as the capital city of the Ottoman Empire. In 1914 , the sole remaining empire that was in Europe consisted of Constantinople (now known as Istanbul) along with the area surrounding it. The Ottomans were humiliated in other areas of the empire too. In the northern part of Africa Egypt was, although nominally still Turkish was still ruled by the British. Libya was recently taken by Italy. The Ottomans still controlled Syria, Palestine, Mesopotamia (Iraq) and Arabia. However, its glory days were over it. It was even referred to as the 'Sick Man in Europe.' However, Turkey was striving to modernize. It was a constitutional republic and had recently passed military reforms.

Tensions, alliances with other countries and international relations

The Great Powers protected their interests through a system of alliances. In 1914, there two blocs of power. The first one was comprised of the Triple Alliance: Germany, Austria-Hungary, and Italy. Germany was wary of the threat of attack from France towards the west, as well as Russia in the eastern region. Austria-Hungary was cautious about Russian plans for the Balkans and also its ties with the tiny Slavic state of Serbia. Serbia has been of great interest to Austria-Hungary. Serbia was a focal point of Slavic patriotic pride, and a lot of Slavs were under the rule of Austro-Hungarian. Austria-Hungary worried that Serbia could be a threat to its fragile empire. This is a crucial consideration when considering the events that led to and triggered the Great War. Austria-Hungary and Germany had formed their alliance on 1879. Italy also joined, but was not a part of the commitment towards the agreement. Italy was a fan of it was the Italian spoken regions in the Austro-Hungarian Empire including the southern region of Tyrol as well as Friuli. In the course of war, Germany, Austria-Hungary and its allies were referred to by the name of Central Powers.

The other major power bloc comprised France, Great Britain and Russia. France was concerned about German ambitions, just as

Germany was suspicious of France. France was also determined to take revenge for it's involvement in Franco-Prussian War and regain Alsace as Lorraine. The policy of Great Britain was to stay in'splendid isolation and to rely on its fleet of powerful ships to defend its own interests. Britain likely feared Russia's plans higher than the Germans. For instance, Russia threatened Britain's interests in India, Afghanistan and Persia and sought control over Constantinople which could have threatened British trade. However, Germany was determined to challenge British control over the oceans which is why the British Government determined that Germany's military needed to be controlled. A deal, known as an "Entente Cordial" was signed by 1904 between France and France during 1904. Russia is concerned about a German and Austro-Hungarian invasion, and determined to protect Serbia and preserve its position in the Balkans made the alliance agreement to France at the end of 1892. In 1907, Russia and Britain formed an entente then in 1907 the Triple Alliance was born. In 1914, these countries and their partners would become the Allies.

The tensions between these alliances were further exacerbated during the period leading up to 1914, which was a number of times. France and German almost fought in the battle over Morocco in 1906 and then again in the year 1911. Between 1912 and 1913,, two wars broke out on two areas of the Balkan Peninsula. They were fought by the Ottoman Empire as well as the smaller Balkan countries Bulgaria, Greece, Montenegro, Serbia and Romania. The Balkan states expanded their territories but mostly at the cost that of their neighbors in the Ottoman Empire. Russia helped Serbia while Austria-Hungary was against Serbia. The other Great Powers intervened with troops but relations between the two alliances were tensions. The wars were generally seen as evidence to the Great Powers had the sense to accept compromises when they realized they were just at the edge of danger.

These tensions led to a fierce arms race. It was the German army was by far the most technologically sophisticated, disciplined and well-equipped. However, the Russian was more powerful. Britain was the most powerful fleet, even though Germany was quickly moving towards. The following table illustrates the amount of the reserve and standing armies for every one of the Great Powers in 1914.

Russia

5971 000

Germany

4500 000

France

4017 000

Austria - Hungary

3000 000

Great Britain

975 000

In July 1914, Europe was like a keg of powder ready to explode. In the majority of people in Europe there was an overwhelming feeling the war would be inevitable. It was just a matter of finding someone to ignite the fire. On the 28th of June 1914, that fuse was ignited by the young Serbian patriot called Gavrilo Princep.

It was the assassination of Franz Ferdinand

The Archduke Franz Ferdinand was a nephew of Emperor Franz Joseph I and heir to the throne of Austria-Hungary in 1914. The Emperor had been through several family tragic events. He was the brother of Maximillian his short reign as the Emperor of Mexico was killed by revolutionary thugs. His wife, the Empress Elizabeth was murdered by anarchists. His son and Crown Prince Rudolf was shot by himself and his lover in 1889. The fate of the Habsburg dynasty was dependent on the heir who was to succeed.

Franz Ferdinand and his wife Duchess Sofie took an official visit in Sarajevo located in Bosnia-Herzegovina. Bosnia-Herzegovina was administered by Austria - Hungary, and was the main source of tension between Austria-Hungary as well as Serbia because there were several Serbs living in the area. It was during this time that the Sarajevo Head of the Police was unhappy with the lack of security measures for such a sensitive trip.

In Sarajevo on the 28th of June Franz Ferdinand and Sophie entered an open car and walked in a motorcade towards Sarajevo town hall. Sarajevo town hall. The royal party was not aware of it. and the security forces only a handful of young Serbian nationalists were preparing to murder the couple. They were members of a secretive and military group known under the name the Black Hand. The motorcade passed by one of them however, he fell off his feet. The motorcade passed the other. Another time, the youngster failed to take action. A little further down the road an additional man hurled bombs towards the Royals' vehicle. The bomb bounced off, fell over the car next to it and detonated, injuring up to 20 people.

Amazingly, it was a surprise that the Archduke along with his spouse walked to the reception in the Town hall. Franz Ferdinand expressed outrage at the incident, but he carried on. The speech he gave to the crowd was stained by the blood of wounded victims. The Archduke's advisers advised him to stay in the town's hall until the troops were able to secure the zone. the Governor general of Bosnia-Herzegovina prohibited the plan on the reason that troops wouldn't have the enough time to change into appropriate uniforms for dress.

Franz Ferdinand decided to change his plans for the remainder of the day, in favor of visiting wounded patients in the hospital. It was determined that the procession should stay clear of the city's center. However , the chauffeur of the car that was royally owned wasn't aware and veered right onto Franz Josef St, veering away from the route planned. From behind the governor-general demanded the driver to turn back. The driver stopped to reverse. While he was waiting an unidentified Serb, Gavrilo Princip, moved forward and from a distance of five feet, fired two shots. The first shot entered the jugular vein of Archduke. The second struck the Duchess Sophie within the abdominal. Franz Ferdinand cried 'Sophie, Sophie! Don't die! Be a role model for your children!

The motorcade made its way to the residence of the governor for medical attention However, Elizabeth was dead upon the time of arrival. Franz Ferdinand died ten minutes later.

Princip was detained together with the others involved in the plot to murder the couple. The reaction to the assassination of Austro-Hungarian's heir as well as his wife was quick. In the Austro -- Hungarian Empire was furious. The Serbs were rioting within Bosnia -

Herzegovina. The entire continent of Europe was stunned. There was shock throughout Europe. Austro the Austro Hungarian Government claimed to have evidence to show that it was Kingdom of Serbia was a major participant in the assassination. The Government on July 23 , demanded on the Serbian Government agree to the demands of a list of ten. These included arresting everyone involved in the assassination, removing all anti-Austro-Hungarian officers from the Serbian military, and allowing Austro-Hungarian officials to supervise the investigation. The demands were too much to meet, especially within the timeframe of forty-eight hours and the imperial administration in Vienna was aware of that.

The role in the involvement of Serbian government isn't in doubt however the extent of involvement is subject to some controversy. Whatever the level of accountability, Austria-Hungary used the situation to degrade Serbia and suppressing the Serbian and southern Slavic the nationalist movements.

Europe is a blunder that leads to war

In the event that the Serbian Government was unable to meet all the demands of Austria-Hungary, the war was declared on July 28. The Russian Government immediately reacted. Serbia was an all-time ally of Russia and Russia did not wish for Austria-Hungary to increase their influence into the Balkans. Tsar Nicholas called for a mobilization troops along the border between Austria and Hungary on the 29th of July. The following day, the mobilization of troops along the German border began. The Kaiser Vilhelm demanded his cousin the Tsar to pull back his troops. The Tsar was not willing to do so. The plans for military were devised by Russian strategists believed that war against Austria-Hungary was the war against Germany too. According to their thinking, the victory was dependent on the mobilization of both nations. So a possibility of avoiding a global war was lost because due to the rigidity Russian plan of action. On August 1st Germany announced war against Russia.

France is bound to its alliance with Russia to come to its assistance. Germany requested France to not. France declined to reply. Germany announced war against France on the 3rd of August.

All eyes were now on Great Britain. What would the British react? Britain was not a member of formal agreements that were formalized with France as well as Russia. The agreement with these countries was more an informal statement of friendship. The reaction of the British Government was based on what was happening in Germany. Before the war , the German had come up with Schlieffen Plan. Schlieffen Plan. In accordance with the plan, most German soldiers would have been positioned on the west. They would then take out France before moving into the eastern region to rejoin with the remaining troops and take on Russia. The plan was based on German armies advancing on France by way of Belgium. The French frontier with Germany was secured with a number of powerful forts. A swift decisive war meant the forts needed to be kept out of.

Today, Belgium is a non-aligned nation and was not a member of either or the Great Powers. In addition the neutrality of Belgium was secured by an international agreement Germany accepted. Britain would not have been able to tolerate the possibility of an invasion by Belgium. Belgian ports were vital for British trade and , in addition, Britain would never have tolerated German ships and troops in Belgium in readiness for an invasion. The last minute prior to war between the two countries of France the kaiser requested to have the German military plan was changed to prevent the possibility of an invasion of Belgium which would have reduced the likelihood of war with Britain. The frightened German generals argued the inability to come up with an entirely new plan within a couple of hours. Vilhelm did not take their advice but another chance to reduce the size of the war went unnoticed. On the 4th of August Germany officially declared war on Belgium after it denied access to military forces. Great Britain declared war later that same day.

Declarations of war welcomed with a way that's impossible to comprehend to us, a hundred years after. A huge crowd were gathered at Vienna, Paris, Berlin, London and St Petersburg. They cheered on the first troops that were off into battle. Women poured over soldiers with flowers and kissed them on the cheeks. Young men lined up to the parade and clergymen spoke on the responsibility of everyone to fight for their country.

There were a few that did not foresee the events to come and mourned the loss of peace. In the days before war, there was a British Foreign Secretary Lord Grey was observing the gas lamps illuminated to light the evening on the street that was beneath his office. He said to a friend"The lamps are being turned off across Europe. We won't see them ever again lit in our lifetimes.'

The "Prisoner of the Vatican is another of the leaders who did not welcome the conflict with enthusiasm. The news of the war sent the pope Pius X, already suffering from heart problems and a weak heart, into a state sadness that lasted for a long time, and from which he was never able to recover. He was Catholic King of Austria-Hungary requested Pius through an emissary to pray for his troops. The pope said "I pray for peace and but not conflict.' Soon after, he was diagnosed with bronchitisand died from an attack of the heart on August 20th. Many believed it to be caused because of the strain of conflict.

The War starts

The leaders of European nations erroneously underestimated how long war would last. The

French believed that they would arrive in Berlin within six weeks, whereas the Germans thought they would arrive in Paris at the same amount of time. The army could move quickly. Railway networks were organized to move huge numbers of troops precisely regards to location and time. The latter part of the nineteenth century, the wars across Europe were swift and with a low number of losses.

The French Army especially is believed to have held to romantic notions of war with magnificent uniforms of cavalry infiltrating enemy lines, and infantry marched in full colour. The French uniform of the infantry of 1914 featured a navy blue jacket with bright red trousers , and a cap. The uniform led to soldiers being easy targets, and many were killed in the process up until the uniform was altered in 1915. However, the uniform was blue, albeit with a lighter shade.

The technological advances that had revolutionized war forever , with two changes specifically. The artillery was advancing rapidly. Cannon was now outclassed by artillery that had massively-barreled guns with enormous power. The Germans were equipped with a howitzer known as "Big Bertha" which could shoot with a distance of twelve and a half miles. Artillery was employed during the Great War to pound the enemies before launching an attack. They punctured the earth with huge holes and then churned the earth to the point that rain would turn battlefields to rivers of mud, in which soldiers were often drowned.

The other weapon that was decisive could be the machine gun. Machine guns had existed for quite a while however, they haven't had the capability of firing at the speed and with such devastating force. They could fire between up to six hundred round per minute. Soldiers who charge enemy lines would be simply mowed down by the enemy, and only a handful of soldiers could actually cross the enemy's lines.

The troops reacted to artillery or Machine gun shots by hiding in trenches. The shovel of a soldier became equally important to his weapon. Armed forces from Europe came into contact and slowed to a standstill. In the aftermath, offensive warfare was replaced with the war of attrition. The warring parties tried to take on each other through heavy artillery firing, poisonous gas, a lack of resources, and propaganda. Battle armor - helmets breast-plates, armored jacketsand even chain mail was brought back. Gas masks were a crucial element of the soldier's kit and bayonets were essential tools during battle. Also, trench mortars and grenades were utilized. Another weapon that was terrifying was the flame-thrower. It was which was used to set fire to people and their surroundings.

However, armies couldn't fight battles in defensive areas. It was still necessary to take ground taken in the event that the enemy wanted to be repelled. That meant that soldiers had be able to leave their trenches and "go over the top' to move across the strip between the enemy trenches, referred to as "No Man's Land", and be at risk of being killed, or wounded through machine gun fire. One or two trenches could be taken during an offensive, but then it could not be. If a win of a lesser magnitude could be won but it was always with a significant loss. Thus, the battlefields turned into slaughterhouses where the children from Europe could be fed.

In the beginning however it was not until at first, the German assault against France went as planned. The tiny Belgian army was unable to withstand the Germans and Germans forces advanced towards Paris. After a first defeat, the French joined forces with British troops British Expeditionary Force (BEF) and held off the Germans in the east of Paris during the Battle of the Marnes (September 5-12) as well as during the Battle of Ypres, the First close to Belgium (October 19 through October 19 to). Along the eastern border, the French started an offensive in Germany however, after their victory at the Battle of Mulhouse (August 20) it came to the ground to.

Then the terrible impasse began to develop with two separate lines battling forces extended across the Flanders coastline all the way to Switzerland. In 1914, the German General Army Erich Von Falkenhayn attempted to cut through his French, British and Belgian lines during the First Battle of Ypres on the 19th of October 1914. The battle lasted for 34 days , and it cost Germans more than 47 000 deaths, compared against the Allies of more than 58 000. Von Falkenhayn was not able to deliver the decisive victory he hoped for. Following the battle, he calmly informed Berlin that Germany would not be able to be victorious and the diplomatic solution must be searched for. He and the Kaiser and his government were not in agreement. However, If Germany was unable to end the deadlock it was also impossible for the Allies.

The battle of Kolubara was fought in Eastern Europe, Austro-Hungarian hopes of a quick victory over Serbia were shattered when Serbia's forces were defeated at the Battles of Cer and Kolubara. It was also the time that Austro - Hungarians also had to confront the Russian invading the region of Galicia which is located in what is today Poland.

The Russians also attacked in the German region in East Prussia and made some advances until they were stopped by the Battle of Tannenberg (August 26 until 30). However, the advance in the Russian army was so alarming for that the Central Powers the Central Powers Germany removed troops to into the Western Front, thus limiting the possibility of a rapid success in France.

However, the prosperity of the Central Powers increased somewhat with the appearance into the Ottoman Empire during the conflict. The Turks were wary of their neighbors, especially the Great Powers, which they blamed for the shrinking of their territories in Europe. They believed Germany could help them fight the Russians as well as the British. A pact of the Emperor and Sultan Mehmed V was agreed to.

On the 29th of October, 1914 Ottoman ships attacked Russian ports along the Black Sea and closed The Dardanelles the narrow strait connecting European as well as Asian Turkey to Allied shipping. The straits were open to all ships and was crucial to Russian trade. The war with Russia brought about another frontier that was located in the Caucasus Mountains, but war with Britain also meant that Britain had combat in Egypt as well.

Despite the inhumanity and horrors of war, towards the close of 1914, there were rays of hope and humanism. 100 British females wrote an unreserved letter to the women from Germany and Austria in a plea for peace. Around the same time Pius X's successor Benedict XV, wrote to the belligerent governments, asking that at Christmas 'the guns might be not be fired, but at the night that the angels sing.' Benedict was also involved for the return of civilians and prisoners of war.

A group of more than 155 German women wrote to their English sisters with the same message, expressing the same desire that humanity prevail. The letter from Benedict was rejected by the authorities. Amazingly, however the pope's request was fulfilled at least in part. At Christmas 1914 and in the week preceding the holiday, soldiers from both sides laid up their arms and crossed over no-man's border, met one another and exchanged greetings and presents. They shared meals, exchanged prisoners and sang Christmas carols, and were even playing football one the other. These truces were observed in both Western as well as the Eastern Fronts. Unfortunately, the military chiefs were able to stop these fraternizations. It is interesting to think about what they might do if the soldiers were simply not willing to fight.

The conflict is getting more intense.

The War in Europe quickly spread to other regions of the world , too. It was a time when the British and French owned vast colonies across Africa, Asia and the Australasia and could mobilize many thousands of soldiers. British India alone provided around 1300 000 soldiers. French as well as British troops entered into the German colony in Togoland as well as Cameroon in Africa in the beginning of August 1914. Then in the Pacific New Zealand occupied German Samoa and Australian troops were able to invade German New Guinea.

The Central Powers as well as the Allies called on all of Europe to join in the battle on their own side. Turkey as we've seen has joined with the Central Powers. Switzerland, Spain, Portugal and Spain, Portugal Netherlands, Sweden, Norway and Denmark all were neutral. It was the United States, lead by President Woodrow Wilson, had also declared neutrality.

The Kingdom of Italy while allies together with Germany and Austria-Hungary but refused to join the alliance and then began secret talks between Great Britain and France. It was the London Pact of April 1915 offered Italy territories of Austro-Hungary that included South Tyrol, Eastern Friuli and Dalmatia. Italy officially declared war on Austria-Hungary on May 23 , 1915. The Italian army wasn't a mighty one when compared with those of the Great Powers, but it mostly fought in Tyrol and Venetia in order to prevent the Austro-Hungarian army from combat along the Eastern Front. The Italians were heavily wounded during battles in the Tyrolean Mountains and also fell short in Venetia. It wasn't until 1918 when they had gained ground.

The Balkans the Balkans countries joined in the war. The tiny Kingdom of Montenegro which was majority Serbian was able to come to Serbia's aid within a couple of days of the declaration of war by Austro-Hungarians. On the 12th of October 1915, Bulgaria was led by the Tsar's government (King) Ferdinand I, was declared a war participant with the Central Powers and was granted a return in exchange for Serbian territory.

In Greece In Greece, King Constantine I favored the Central Powers however, he was determined to ensure that Greece from joining the conflict. The prime minister of his government Eleftherios Venizelos wanted Greece to be part of the Allies and he invited 15 000 French or British troops to arrive at the harbor of Salonika and make it an operational base to fight Austria - Hungary and Bulgaria. The Allies started landing on the 3rd of October 1915.

Constantine removed Venizelos as a king, and Venizelos' supporters staged a coup attempt to take over the King. The rebellion failed, however, Venizelos set up a rival government in the city of Thessalonika, in October 1916. He was aided by Allied forces. Venizelos was in charge for the military of Thessalonika's royalist army as well as navy. However, Greece remains divided. Constantine who was supported by the Russian government, remained as the throne's holder. He abdicated only at the end of June in 1917. Then, shortly afterwards, Greece declared war on the Central Powers.

It was a Kingdom of Romania was ruled by the House of Hohenzollern, which was a part from the family which was the ruler of the German Empire in addition, Carol I was pro-German. However, the majority of people were for supporting the Allied cause. Romania was willing to fight for the Allies in exchange for the Romanian spoken lands in Transylvania in Hungary declaring war the 27th, 1916. Romania's Romanian army was among the largest of the Balkans with a total of 700 000 soldiers.

Portugal and Germany jointly declared war on the 9th of March 1916 in response to British pressuring Portugal's Portuguese government. More than 60 000 Portuguese soldiers fought on Western Front.

The war also extended across further Far East. In the 19th century, the nations of Europe and including the United States and Japan (principally Great Britain, Russia, Germany, France and Japan) were able to force territory and concessions, or leases, of in the Chinese Empire, making the Chinese Empire vulnerable and disgraced. In 1914 in 1914, it was the Japanese Empire was an emerging industrialized country that overcome the Russian Empire during the Russo-Japanese War of 1904 to 1906, and also defeated its less powerful neighbor China during the Sino-Japanese War from 1894 to 1895. In the second war, it had acquired Korea in addition to Formosa. From the first, it had seized the crucial surrender to Port Arthur (Lushunkou).

Japan was a key all-weather ally for Great Britain in the Pacific and saw an opportunity to expand the influence of its country in China by grabbing its German concessions. It declared war against Germany on August 23, 1914 and against Austria-Hungary on August 25, 1914. Japan quickly took over all of the German concessions, with the naval base at Tsingtao being the most important.

After the success it had over Germany, Japan presented China with a list of 21 demands. They demanded that China surrender huge portions of Chinese territory and to the extent that China could have become an independent state of Japan. The revolution of 1848 had overthrown the previous Manchu Emperor, Pu Yi, and the new Chinese republic was shattered by internal discord. China was forced into a concession to any and all of demands. A fury about Japan and the desire to get rid of any influence from outside convinced the China's leaders China to declare war against Germany on August 14, 1917. They were hoping for China to be a participant in peace talks and to make its position. However, China didn't get its goals. When the war came to an end, Allied powers were more favorable to Japan over China and concessions were not reaffirmed.

The First World War involved the Americas as well. The involvement by America's United States of America will be examined in a future chapter, but in addition to all the American belligerents, it is possible to list Brazil, Nicaragua, Honduras, Costa Rica, Haiti, Cuba, Guatamala and Panama. Of those the five, the only one was Brazil. Brazil had troops in Europe.

In the course of the conflict, twenty-three nations participated for both sides. Allied side. There were 15 states who were fighting on behalf of the Central Powers (some of these included Poland, Lithuania and the Ukraine were derived from territories that were conquered). Twenty-four countries were, at the very least neutral. The majority of manpower as well as economic assets was evidently at the disposal of the Allied powerhouses.

Chapter 16: The Progress Of The War 1915-1916

In the Western Front the German advance was stopped by the close of 1914. In 1916, the Germans started another offensive against Verdun, a fortress city. Verdun located on the River Meuse, in the west of France. Verdun was the largest fortification in France. The fort was flanked by a number of forts that were less powerful but still powerful. If Verdun was captured, Verdun could be a significant gain , but also a catastrophic loss for France. General Erich Von Falkenhayn launched an attack with 130 000 troops. Initially, the Germans advanced against 30 000 French defenses However, reinforcements came in and the attack was stopped. Both sides fed thousands of soldiers into the battle. In the midst of the war that lasted from February 21 through December 18, nearly two million soldiers were fighting, the strength of both sides being about equal.

After 303 days and nearly 1 million casualties, French retained Verdun. However, Falkenhayn justifies the war in his memoir following the war. After deciding during 1914 the conflict was not winnable through a conventional war and he set out to bring France to smithereens in a battle of attrition. His aim was to "bleed France to white.'

The Allies also began offensives to break through the German line and to force them to withdraw. A string of offensives in 1915 were met with only a small or no results. In the aftermath of Verdun the British general in charge general Douglas Haig, observed that Falkenhayn's strategy of destroying France appeared to work. The general therefore decided to go on an offensive with British troops to ease the tensions over the French. The attack was to become the famous bloodbath referred to in historians in the form of Battle of the Somme.

The River Somme offensive in northwestern France started on July 1 following an entire week of heavy rain along with the subsequent mud. War planes played a significant part in the battle. They were primarily used for reconnaissanceand equipped with machine guns that could bring down the aircraft of enemy. The Somme also witnessed the first tanks being used. The armoured vehicles were designed by the Allies to assist in solving the deadlock. They were able to travel across rough terrain, such as trenches, and also provide support to infantry. While they were able to be deployed to the greatest advantage, they were mechanically inefficient, heavy and slow (most could only move at a walk speed). It wasn't till World War II that the tank became the essential weapon of offense as it is nowadays. In a way, the Germans who would later be the best at tank warfare during the Second World War, were not impressed with them during The Great War and built few of them.

It was reported that the British and French returned to only 8 kilometers of French soil before the offensive was stopped on the 18th of November. These few kilometers cost the British the 420 000 soldiers. They also lost 200 000. French suffered losses of 200 000. Germany was hit with between the 430 000-500 000 losses.

If the Somme did anything, it was possibly the realization by the side of Germany that Falkenhayn, who was dismissed in the course of battle was correct throughout. Germany did not take on the world. The views of survivors can be summarized by an German official, Friedrich Steinbrecher: 'Somme. The entire history of the globe cannot contain a more horrific word.'

In the spring of 1916, an uprising with guns took place in Ireland that was at the time during British rule. Germany was providing the rebels with weapons. They were repelled easily and with great ferocity. In the end, the Easter Rising hastened Irish independence but still evokes emotions that are still strong today.

At the Eastern Front the initial successes of the Russian forces were becoming reversed. They were Russian Army was massive, but was poorly-equipped, poorly trained, and led by unqualified officers. Food and clothing were frequently lacking as were weapons. In the mid-1915s, it was clear that the Central Powers had forced their Russians away from Alicia and had occupied Russian Poland. Tsar Nicholas II was able to respond to the disasters by assuming the personal charge of all the military forces, a post to which he was totally not suited. However, his Brusilov Offensive, named after General Alexei Brussilov, was initially successful and made progress across Poland in 1914 and Galicia during 1916. However, the Russians did not sustain the gains. The losses in the field sparked tensions within the country. People suffering from the burden of conflict, protested. The Duma demanded change. The Tsar started to feel himself becoming more and more alone. He didn't realize that both he as well as his Romanoff administration were in danger.

In 1915, Serbia and Montenegro lost to Austro-Hungarian as well as Bulgarian troops.

The conflict at sea

Control over the oceans was crucial in the First World War for both sides. Whoever was in charge of the sea lanes, they managed trade. They also controlled trade. British as well as French fleets were utilized to block German and Austro and Austro Hungarian ports, cutting off supplies to fight the war and to ensure morale in the home. The German navy made just one attempt to break through the blockade. It was a battle between the German as well as British fleets clashed at Jutland on the coast of Denmark in June, 1916. Admiral Jellicoe led the Grand Fleet comprising the 151 warships. Admiral Reinhard Scheer was in charge of 99 ships in the High Seas Fleet. The Battle was fought until June 1 and was the biggest naval battle in the First World War.

After the smoke had gone out, it was clear that the British had lost 14 warships and nearly 7000 men, in comparison to Germany's eleven vessels and 3000 men. Both sides claimed victory. The Germans had won on the technical level but the British claimed they been victorious by preventing the break blocksades. It was the last time that such huge fleets fight in the course of the war or afterward.

However, if the Allies were more powerful on the seas , the Germans represented a risk under it. The German submarine, also known as an "unterseeboot" (U-boat) was a potent tool to defend Allied shipping. Between October 1916 until January 1917, German U-boats were able to sink eleven million tonnes of goods of the allied and numerous merchant ships along with their crews. The use of escorts in order to protect merchant vessels hindered their effectiveness in the u-boat war. The decision of 1917 to allow u-boats attack any shipping vessel, Allied or neutral compelled the United States to enter the war.

Warships could also be used to assist transports of troops. In April 1915, French as well as British ships carried around 500 000 soldiers, mostly of Britain, Ireland, and Australia and up to Dardanelles. Dardanelles Dardanelles was a stretch of ocean that separated European Turkey (Thrace) from Asia. Winston Churchill, then First Lord of the Admiralty and a member of the Admiralty, had suggested for an attack on the Dardanelles. This would create a route of supplies to Russia as well as permit Allied troops to strike Constantinople.

The battle was among the worst executed and planned operations of the war. The first attack by the navy was unsuccessful. The Allied troops that landed on the beachheads were crushed by 300000 Turkish troops firing from the cliffs they were expected to go up against the cliffs. The battle, named in honor of the Gallipoli Peninsula costs each side around 250 000 dollars, of that 46000 Allies along with 65 000 Turks suffered deaths. In the month of January 1916, after nine months of fighting the Allied troops retreated.

1917. The United States and Russia

The year 1917 was upon us and neither side appeared more en route in winning this war. However, in 1917 it was the year that United States entered the war as a member of the Allies and the crumbling Romanoff regime fell to the ground in Russia. Both events had major effects on the battle field.

In 1914, the public was largely for neutrality. The president Woodrow Wilson was strongly for neutrality and saw himself as a potential peace broker.

In 1915, public opinion changed. On May 1 , 1915, The British liner Lusitania set sail from New York for Liverpool. Before leaving it, the German Embassy located in Washington had put this notice in several American newspapers:

Notice!

Travelers planning for the Atlantic journey should be informed that a state of war is in place in the region between Germany with her allies, and Great Britain and her allies The zone of war encompasses the waters that border the British Isles; that, as per the formal notice provided to the Imperial German Government, vessels fly the flag of

Germany and her allies are allowed to sail in the area.

Of Great Britain, or any of her allies, are susceptible to destruction in the waters. Those who sail in the area of war on ships belonging to Great Britain or her allies take part on their own responsibility.

Imperial German Embassy

Washington, D.C., 22 April 1915.

On May 7 , the Lusitania was struck by an German U-boat off the shores of Ireland. It was leaving New York and was bound to Liverpool. The passengers included 1962 who comprised 1266 civilian passengers. A torpedo hit the ship in the bow to the starboard. It was then that the Lusitania began to shake and it became difficult to launch her lifeboats. In actual, only six of forty-eight launched. A few of the ones that were launched sank or broke.

After 18 minutes of the torpedo struck it was discovered that the bow vessel was able to hit the seabed with the stern remaining above the surface. Within a few minutes, the stern was also submerged to the deepest depths.

The British cruise ship Juno located in Cork and rushed to help and although its crew did their best to save many, 1198 died. Similar to the Titanic catastrophe five years prior many of the passengers and crew members were lost to the freezing waters.

Around the world, the sinking was condemned as a sly attack on unarmed vessels for civilians. Germany declared that it had the legal right to strike Lusitania because it was carrying military-related supplies (which the ship was). One hundred and thirty nine passengers were US citizens, while one hundred and twenty-eight of them were dead. The furore in this country United States pushed that country closer to war. But Wilson was not ready to declare war on the country by launching a protest and demanding compensation for the family members of the deceased.

Some historians have claimed that the circumstances that led to Lusitania's sinking Lusitania were quite bizarre. What did it do in waters which were well-known for u-boat activity particularly when it was advised by the German diplomatic embassy? 23 merchant vessels had been lost in the area. What do we take from a letter sent by Winston Churchill, the First Lord of the Admiralty addressed to Walter Runciman, President of the British Board of Trade, where he states "It is essential to bring neutral ships to our shores, in the hope of especially encroaching with the United States with Germany .... The more you can get, and if a portion of it is in trouble Better yet'. Communication among Lusitania along with Lusitania and the British Admiralty remain secret until this day.

The relations between United States and the German Empire worsened following the Zimmerman Telegram scandal. In the month of January 1917, the German Foreign Minister, Arthur Zimmerman, sent an encrypted telegram to Mexican Government. The message was intercepted by the British Government, decoded and sent to the United States. In the cable, he explains that Germany believes that war against America is United States is, while not wanted, inevitable since they Imperial

Government intends to allow its u-boats the right to attack any vessel with no restrictions. He suggests the formation of an alliance Germany and Mexico suggesting that Mexico is annexed to territories taken from Mexico through the United States in the nineteenth century, namely, Texas, New Mexico and Arizona.

The Mexican Government responded, very rightly and in a very logical manner, that Mexico did not have a chance of winning an actual war with America. United States, and Mexico was neutral throughout the remainder period of war. However, the release of the telegram ignited the anti-German and anti-Mexican sentiments. This was especially so because US troops were crossing the Mexican border in response to attacks on New Mexico by the revolutionary Pancho Villa. Yet, some voices from the British-dominated part of the US mostly with German and Irish origin, believed that the telegram was a fake. This was disproved by Zimmerman himself, who claimed that it was true in the belief that Americans would be able to understand that their country's attempt to keep out conflict.

Woodrow Wilson believed he could be inactive for a while. Wilson pleaded with Congress to declare war against Germany. On April 6 , 1917, Congress declared an emergency state of war against Germany. The 17th of December was the day that Congress declared the war against Austria-Hungary. Wilson justification was that the war was going to be a war that would be the end of all conflict' and could make the world safe for democracy'. These are words that resonate, and many claim to be hollow even to this day.

The United States sent four million soldiers to war, most of them in the Western Front. In the war under the command of General John Pershing, they arrived at an average of 10000 per day, bringing the much-needed relief, assistance and equipment for British as well as French troops.

While in Russia the conflict caused widespread discontent. There was a severe shortage of food and other items both in Russia and overseas. It was clear that the Turkish blocking of Dardanelles was denying Russia of commerce. The Empire's economy was largely agricultural and it was not capable of producing weapons to the level that Other Great Powers could. Inflation was prevalent. In 1917, the price of goods had increased by fourfold. Farmers who were peasants kept their crops in order to provide for themselves, making cities were starving.

The Empire was tired of war, and the initially enthusiasm of the government was beginning to fade. Tsar Nicholas II was unaware of this. He was ostracized from the demands of his people, he acted on his belief that God was God's representative on Earth He believed they were loyal to him. He seemed to be completely unaware of the harm one individual specifically caused towards the Romanoffs.

Grigori Rasputin was monk who gained remarkable influence over the family of the Tsar and, in particular, over the Empress Alexandra. He earned a reputation for a saint and was soon circulating in the circles of the aristocratic. In 1905, he was introduced to the Tsar. Alexandra was convinced by a close friend to seek the help of Rasputin for her child, Alexei. He was born 1904 Alexei had haemophilia an extremely debilitating illness that affected a lot of members of European royals. Prince Leopold the younger son of Queen Victoria was afflicted as do four other grandchildren as well as the six great-grandchildren of Queen Victoria. It is believed that the Queen Victoria was carrying the chromosome that is linked to the illness, even however, she was not diagnosed by haemophilia. Alexei was the great-grandson of Victoria.

Haemophilia interferes with the capacity for the body create blood clots. Haemophilia sufferers bleed longer than the rest of us. Alexei was often in extreme discomfort due to internal bleeding. His mother believed that Rasputin could help his condition. There is a suggestion that the most Rasputin did was inform the Empress that she should allow Alexei restand allow him to recover naturally. Whatever the treatment is, Rasputin gained influence over the Empress and, through her, the Tsar. Additionally, Rasputin confirmed the Tsar in his belief that he was ruled by divine law and advised him to resist demands for reform.

It was the dependence of the family of the royals this monk sparked outrage in the society. The critics criticized Rasputin's lechery as well as his drinking. He said he could only attain the grace of salvation through indulgence in depravity. It was alleged that he was sexing with aristocratic ladies as a reward for spiritual favours. The story was that his raped a nun. Both the wife of his Tsar were ignorant of this.

In 1916, a group of nobles, headed by the Prince Felix Yusopov and the Grand-duke Dmitri Pagolovich, plotted to murder Rasputin. On December 20, Rasputin was invited to an dinner party at the Yusopov Palace in Petrograd (now known as St Petersburg). The conspirators served him desserts and wine with huge amounts of the cyanide. The fact that cyanide didn't affect Rasputin is now a legend. Astonished, Yusupov shot him through the back using the revolver. The assassins fled and assumed he was dead. Then, Yusopov returned to check on the body. Rasputin began to open his eyes. He sat up to his feet, swung at Yusupov and began to beat him. After hearing the noise, the other conspirators came in and fired at Rasputin at least three times on the back. Rasputin fell to the ground. When the men walked towards him, He struggled to stand up. It was amazing to realize that he was alive. Yusupov and the other gang members hit Rasputin until he died. Then they wrapped the body of Rasputin in a blanket and threw it into frigid River Neva.

A few days later, the remains of Rasputin was taken by the river. An autopsy determined it was the result of due to cyanide. The deceased was not killed by shooting injuries. The numerous clubbings have not killed the man. He drowned.

The demise of Rasputin made the Empress Alexandra with a sense of loss. Nicholas was a fragile and unsure at worst of times, did not have the spiritual guidance that he required. In the frontline, Russian army, tired and hungry, with no supplies, were retreating. There were demonstrations throughout Petrograd, Moscow and other cities to protest the shortage of bread. In the meantime, Russian Secret Police warned government officials that the public turmoil would soon be uncontrollable. It was the Duma advised Nicholas that without reform and the constitution to be truly democratic the regime would collapse. The Tsar totally ignored the warnings.

On February 8, 1917, people (both males and females) protested in street demonstrations in the capital city of Petrograd and demanded bread. On March 10, they were joined by most of the city's students and employees of the city. The next day, the Tsar instructed the garrison in Petrograd to suppress what he believed was an unrest even though very few were calling for that the government end. The troops were unable to agree to this and socialists within the city were permitted to form an Soviet ('council') to represent the soldiers and workers. The Duma accepted Petrograd Soviet as the Petrograd Soviet as a legitimate organization and formed a partnership it to establish a temporary government.

After hearing the announcement that the Tsar Nicholas set off for Petrograd but, when he arrived at Pskov which was 290 km from the capital and the Duma as well as the chief of the Army, Nikolai Ruzsky, demanded that he abdicate. Realizing the gravity in the present, Nicholas abdicated the throne not only for himself but also for the son of his Alexei. The document of abdication on the 15th of March 1917. It was the end of the Romanoff regime. Romanoff regime had been in power for over 300 years. It was over by the pen stroke.

After his abdication , the Tsar was put under house arrest along with his family members at his palace in Tsarskoye Selo, not far from Petrograd. Nicholas was keen for to allow his son Grand Duke Michael to succeed to the throne, however, Michael refused because he was concerned for his own safety.

It was unwieldy and divisive. It was divided and weak. Duma along with the Petrograd Soviet had a battle to be the top control. The government was initially led by Prince Lvov and later through Alexander Kerensky. The Allied powers accepted this new administration and worried to see Russia continued to fight.

The the neutral Switzerland the one Vladimir Lenin was watching these events with great fascination. Lenin was revolutionary, who had fled Russia prior to the conflict. He was a well-known Bolshevik and an wing of Marxists. Lenin believed in the use of violence to attain goals that were revolutionary. He also believed that the war between Germany in addition to Austria-Hungary is an imperialist struggle which could not further Marxism. Marxism. Lenin wanted to travel to Russia however his entry was prevented by Germany. The German authorities were pleased to arrange his secure passage, hoping they could overthrow the Provisional Government and make peace with the Central Powers.

Arriving in Petrograd in the month of April 1917 Lenin immediately slammed Petrograd's Provisional Government as imperialist. Lenin reorganized the Bolshevik party into a powerful force. At this point, the interim government was in crisis. There were protests by peasants and demands for reforms to land. In cities, workers participated in strikes in the hope of immediate changes. Workers and soldiers across the nation were taking part in demonstrations in a chant of 'end the war' and demanding the removal of the soviets which had been forming all across Russia.

The unrest grew worse after the devastating Kerensky Offensive in July 1917. Russians engaged in Galicia and were met with intense resistance, despite early victories. Sixty thousand Russian soldiers were killed or taken prisoner. Despair spread across the ranks. Soldiers wouldn't be fighting until having debated what they thought was the best way to implement their commanders and their orders. A lot of them were unwilling to fight. The Russian offensive was defeated and Russian forces were repelled into the Ukraine.

On the 17th of July, a protest of 500 000 soldiers as well as employees in Petrograd demanded the transfer control of Petrograd from the Provisional Government to the soviets. Lenin as well as his Bolsheviks were able to stand with the protests. The government arrested the top leaders of the Bolsheviks however Lenin fled into hiding. The government issued an order to the army to assume control of Petrograd However, the Bolsheviks along with other socialist parties pushed the army to resign.

Influence of Lenin and the Bolsheviks was gaining momentum during the Soviets. On the 25th of October, 1917, the Bolsheviks were the main force behind a revolt towards the Kerensky Government and seized the Winter Palace, former home of the Tsar, and today the official residence of the government. On the morning of the 26th of October Kerensky had left Petrograd as the Bolsheviks had declared victory. In the end, Soviet Union had been born.

The new administration almost immediately began talks to Germany and Austria-Hungary to bring the war to an end. Lenin was eager to organize the country and was ready to agree to peace at any time. A peace treaty was signed and negotiations began.

The German conditions were harsh. Russian Poland was set to be an independent state within Germany along with the Ukraine as well as those of the Baltic States comprised of Lithuania, Latvia and Estonia. Lenin was willing to accept the idea the idea, but a lot of his fellow colleagues opposed. The breakdown of negotiations resulted in a reprise of hostilities as well as further advances to Russian territory. In response, the Central Powers provided peace with even more savage conditions that were discussed prior to. Lenin accepted and the Treaty of Brest-Litovsk (Brest) was signed on March 3 , 1918.

However, it is true that Lenin believed that he had purchased peace for Russia the truth was that he was wrong. The various factions who were dispossessed by the Bolesheviks such as capitalists, monarchists republicans, monarchists - started organizing themselves and armed against the Soviets. These rebel forces are supported with Allied forces. The Allies were determined to destroy the Soviets and bring Russia to reenter the war. The newly-created States comprising Ukraine, Poland, Finland, Belarus, Lithuania, Latvia, Estonia, and other states, joined. The forces of these states were collectively referred to by the name of Whites. The soviets reacted and created their own Red Army. This Russian Civil War last from 1917 until 1923, and ended with victory for Bolesheviks but with the price of 3 million wounded and dead on both sides.

As these events took place, the Tsar Nicholas as well as his entire family were in prison, and the question was how to deal with the prisoners. The British Government offered to take them in, but the decision was later changed due to pressure from Nicholas's uncle, George V. George V. The British were concerned the presence of their prisoners in Britain could incite a rise in revolutionary sentiment. After the Bolsheviks were in power in 1917 and civil war began, there was speculation of there was a chance that the White Army would rescue them and restore the monarchy. In fact the Romanoffs themselves have believed that it would happen.

In April 1918, the Bolsheviks relocated to the Romanoffs into Yekaterinburg within Yekaterinburg in the Ural Mountains, ironically named in honor of Yekaterinburg, the home of Tsar Peter the Great who established Petrograd (then known as St Petersburg), the powerful capital city of the Romanoff empire. On the 17th of July, the family was awakened around 2.00 am, and told they were going to be relocated to the basement to ensure their security, as White forces were located just from Yekaterinburg. Nicholas, Alexandra, Alexei as well as daughters Olga, Maria, Tatiana and Anastasia were taken down together with their doctor footman, cook and maid. In the adjoining room was a group of ten soldiers accompanied by the Bolshevik leader, Yakov Yorovsky.

When she was in the basement Alexandra noticed that there no chairs. Two people were brought into the room. Alexandra and Alexei who were taken down by Nicholas was in a chair. Then , the soldiers poured into. Yurovsky explained to them all that they were sentenced to execution in authorities of the Ural Soviet. Then, Nicholas cried 'what? What?' Then he returned to his family. The soldiers began firing in a chaotic fashion. Yurovsky shot the former Emperor of Russia multiple times on the chest. Alexandra suffered a gunshot to the head after she tried to tie herself. Alexis was shot in the head. Alexis was shot and was stabbed with the bayonet. If he survived, he was struck into the skull. The girls were able to survive the initial storm of bullets. Diamonds placed in their clothes protected the girls, but they were slain to death by bayonets. Anna Demidova, the maid tried to protect herself by using a pillow filled with diamonds and gems however, she was killed by bayonets.

When the bodies were taken out on stretchers One girl, perhaps Anastasia and possibly Anastasia, began crying. The girl was then stabbed several times and shot.

In 1998, the bodies were extracted from the surface of a dirt road in Yekaterinburg. They were buried inside St Peter and Paul Cathedral in St Petersburg. The guest at the service was prince Michael of Kent who was representing his part of the British royal Family.

On August 14, 2000, The Tsar's family and the rest of his clan were declared as saints in the Russian Orthodox Church.

The alleged escape of Anastasia has turned into the stuff of legends. A minimum of ten women are believed to be Anastasia but none have been verified and no one from the larger Romanoff clan has believed in her existence. There has been speculation that she disappeared in the midst of the funerals belonging to the Romanoff family were taken away. The account of Anastasia crying as she was being removed probably fuelled the speculations. DNA tests have however determined one of Anastasia's bodies to be that of Anastasia.

The Western Front

As we've observed, the ability of Germany to strike was exhausted by 1916. Generals Hindenburg and Ludendorff were replaced by Falkenhayn. They established a line defense that is known as the Hindenburg Line. In the months of February through April 1917 the Germans were on a retreat of about fifty kilometers along the line. The defensive positions narrowed the front and made it more manageable to hold.

On June 7 , that year , the British took on in the Hindenburg Line in the Flanders Offensive. General Douglas Haig argued for the campaign, which was opposed by David Lloyd -George, Prime Minister of Great Britain, and the French general Ferdinand Foch. The rationale behind embarking on an offensive especially after the defeat of a similar battle in Flanders only four months before. But there was a consensus that the British War Cabinet approved the offensive on July 25.

Haig and Haig and his French as well as Belgian counterparts assaulted The city in Ypres in July 31 which began the battle that is now known as the 3rd Battle of Ypres and the battle of Passchendaele. As was the norm it was the Allies started the assault with artillery fire on German positions. Three thousand artillery guns fired 4,500,000 rounds that turned soil into coarse clay. The assault of the infantry across the deserted areas followed. The next thing that happened was the largest downpour that the region had seen in the past thirty years. The clay that was churned became dirt, blocking tanks and rifles, and drowning people and horses.

Mustard gas was a gruesome weapon employed in this war. It was just recently made available and used on both sides although the Allies first began using it in the month of November 1917. It can cause blistering and burning blindness and, when breathed in internally, bleeding. Even though it is prohibited by international law it was used recently by certain soldiers.

The attack was unsuccessful, but however re-enacted two weeks after. After about a month of fighting, Allied forces managed to take a hill to the southeast of Ypres and the destroyed remnants of the town of Passchendaele. Haig was able to use this as a reason to stop the war however, history will consider the attack as another in the list of failed campaigns during the Great War. Together, Allied and German deaths were close to one million. Lloyd-George described Passchendaele one of the greatest mistakes during the conflict. ... There is no soldier of any kind supports this illogical campaign.'

Falkenhayn's dream of 'bleeding France white' appeared to be near to being fulfilled in 1917. The French were the ones who suffered the most of the conflict. Of the twenty million French males who were fighting 1 million of them had perished during battle. This meant that the French Army was weakened and lost the capability and the desire to fight. The French were worried by the French were on the verge of breaking.

On May 3, the French Second Division received instructed to assault the enemy's lines. The division did not agree. It retreated from the weapons it was carrying, however it did not surrender. The end of May 27000 soldiers refused to fight. The rebellion continued through June and , by the time it was over, 50% of the Army had joined in a mutiny. The news about the Russian Revolution was spreading among the soldiers. Russian army soldiers fighting in the Western Front were encouraging their French friends to uproot their rulers. Russian soldiers were not willing to fight. Why should the soldiers of France?

The mutiny was quickly quelled. There were a few executions, however, the President of France, Raymond Poincare, and General Philippe Petain were anxious to restore morale. They pledged longer vacation and a halt to major attacks.

In the context of this depressing situation, one could imagine the two sides are willing to engage in talks of peace. Following The Battle of Verdun at the close of 1916, Germany offered to negotiate to they offered to mediate, and the United States offered to mediate. This was prior to the time that when the United States declared war and prior to there was even the Zimmermann incident. As a peacemaker, a position that he'd always aspired to, Wilson asked both sides to express their demands. Germany did not accept Wilson's mediation, preferring to address those Allied nation directly. The Allies required the removal of all the territories held by Central Powers, war reparations as well as the establishment of a sovereign Polish state, as well as guarantees to stop future wars. This could have been the basis for negotiations however, the Germans were unable to come up with specific requirements that were their own. Therefore, the negotiations ended.

Another peace initiative came out in August 1917. It was this time via the Vatican. It was Pope Benedict XV proposed a peace plan based upon seven points:

The'moral force of law was intended to substitute for the force of arms.

Mutual disarmament.

A mechanism to facilitate international arbitration';

The sea's freedom.

No war indemnities.

The removal of territories was not a matter of contention between the two sides.

The validity of rival claims will be examined.

This kind of proposal could serve as the basis that allows peace to be achieved in every scenario and at any time however, the idea is rejected by both Central Powers as well as the Allies. The pope was seen by both sides as biased towards the other.

So the slaughter carried on.

1918 - The conclusion

The demise of Russia and the peace of Brest-Litovsk that took place in March 1917 had profound implications to both Central Powers and the Allies. The tens of millions of German soldiers were now at liberty to fight on Western Front. In the spring of 1918, General Ludendorf started an offensive. This marked the very first significant German attack since Verdun the year 1916. The plans were bold. Ludendorf wanted to disarm the downhearted French and capture Paris and bring an end to the conflict.

The German advance started on the 21st of March and was met with huge victory. The German troops, joined by easterly troops, expanded as much up to sixty kilometers. The Germans hadn't advanced this many miles in the Western Front since 1914. The Germans were within 120 km of Paris and German artillery bombarded Paris. Germans in frontline and in their homes were overjoyed. Victory was close. The Kaiser announced an official holiday in honor of.

However, the Germans made a mistake. They had advanced fast and far. The troops were not sufficiently supplied with food and water. It was reported that the British and French had suffered damage but not broken. New troopers from United States were daily on the road towards the front. The Germans were overextended. The Germans were tired, depleted of resources and were without reinforcements. The war had killed their most effective soldiers. In August, the Allies attacked. In the Battle of Amiens on August 8th, also known as the 'Black day for the German Army', the Germans started to retreat towards their positions along the Hindenburg Line. In announcing that he would not be victorious in the battle and talks with Allies should begin Ludendorff offered his resignation to the Kaiser Vilhelm. The Kaiser was unable to accept it.

On the 13th of August, the German High Command and the Imperial Government agreed that the war was not winnable. Austria and Hungary stated that they could not endure any longer than December. Austria is Hungary had stopped fighting the

Russians However, the Italians were making progress in the meantime. Allies had conquered Serbia as well as Bulgaria in Greece. In 1916 Franz Joseph had died. He was the new the Emperor of Austria and the King of Hungary was Franz Joseph's great-grandnephew, Charles I. He was confronted by the difficult task of maintaining his Habsburg Empire intact, despite the ferocious and seemingly insoluble tensions between its citizens.

In a address to members of the United States Congress, Woodrow Wilson was announcing 'Fourteen points that could be the basis for the peace treaty could be signed on the 8th of January. These points comprised the freedom of trade as well as the seas, disarmament and the establishment of an international organization to keep peace and recognition of the right to independence for all nations. Some of these were identical to or similar to the ideas from Benedict XV. On the 14th of September, Emperor Charles I wrote to all belligerents a letter asking for peace talks on neutral territory and using as a basis the Fourteen Points as a basis. He was willing to turn his empire to a union of autonomous staring. On the next day Germany also demanded talks with an neutral Netherlands.

The Allied powers resisted both demands. They knew it was obvious that it was obvious that the Central Powers were at the verge of collapse as well France, Great Britain and Italy were in a position of requesting the conditions they desired.

First of all the Central Powers to capitulate was Bulgaria on September 29, 1918. The Ottoman Empire came in on the 30th of October. A joint Italian and French -- British victory in the Battle of Vittorio Veneto in the eastern part of Italy was the final blow of the Austro-Hungarian empire. While it was the Imperial government was seeking to negotiate an armistice,, the Austro-Hungarian Empire was able to be a reality. Hungary was able to break away from its association with Austria. In the meantime, Czechs, Slovaks and southern Slavs all declared their independence. The armistice that was signed on November 3 was done on behalf of an empire becoming an empty shell. In November, Charles I renounced his authority (though not his crown) and acknowledged the rights of each nation to determine the destiny of its people.

In the year 1945, the German government was in desperate need of peace. Following it was reported that German High Command informed the Kaiser that the situation was not a good one in addition to the fact that Allies might break through the German boundaries at any point and that the Kaiser's government had sent a letter at Woodrow Wilson requesting an armistice that was based on the president's Fourteen Points. Wilson responded on the 23rd of October by stating that the Germans should first pull out of Belgium and other territories that were occupied, stop U-boat attacks, and then take the necessary steps to forcibly Vilhelm II to quit. In the end, Germany might be forced to surrender, and not negotiating peace.

These terms, including the surrender of the kaiser and surrender, were not accepted by the military leadership and General Ludendorff, who was the one who had previously declared to the kaiser that the war was over, advocated fighting until the end. But, the soldiers were eager to return home, and desertions were common with the exception of the most adolescent and smallest of recruits did not show up and the troops were in desperate need of supplies. In the end, the Imperial Government sacked Ludendorff and returned to talks. Finally, the Allies agreed to armistice negotiations with an additional clause was added. In the end, Germany must pay compensation, which would mean that it had to acknowledges the responsibility of the conflict.

In the meantime, the German government began to collapse. In the hopes that this could bring about the Allies more tolerant of peace the German government Germany was freed from the influence by the militaries and put directly on the shoulders of the democratically elected Reichstag. However, it was too little and too late to save the beleaguered government.

On the 24th of October on the 24th of October, the German naval fleet received orders into the sea to confront with the British Royal Navy. It was believed that the Imperial Government believed that a last attack could be able to break the Allied blockade and grant Germany the ability to negotiate at negotiations for peace. This was a desperate move that had a slim chance of succeeding. The German sailors refused to follow the orders. They resisted in Port Vilhemshaven on the 29th of October. A mutiny in Kiel's main port for naval vessels in Kiel came just a few days after.

The news of the uprising was quickly spread, and was backed by German Social Democratic Party, Communists and Trade Unions. Workers councils and soldiers similar to the Soviets in Russia were formed and the support from Russia was evident. Governments of numerous German states that comprised the Empire were dissolved and their dynastic rulers were removed.

The head of the Social Democrats was Friedrich Ebert. Despite his disdain for the system, the monarchist he was and the Prince Maximillian as the Chancellor believed that they could collaborate in order to preserve the empire however, on more of a progressive and liberal social foundation. However, it became apparent to both of them that the kaiser needed to step down.

In all of this period Vilhelm II had not been even in Berlin. He was instead at Command Headquarters at Spa, not even realizing that he was losing control over the situation. Prince Maximillian contacted him to explain what was going on and convince him to quit. The Kaiser was not willing to do so. He hoped to be able to save the crown by personally leading his troops back to the front. They might not be with a victory but that would have been a demonstration of unity with his soldiers. Wilhelm believed that control of the army was with the military. The military, however, had realized that they were no longer in control. In frustration, the chancellor returned to Berlin and declared that the kaiser abdicated , despite the fact that it was the 9th of November. After noticing that the decision was taken for the sake of him, Vilhelm formally abdicated and was forced to leave the Netherlands which was then his son, the Crown Prince Vilhelm.

In contrast to the Tsar Nicholas II, unlike Tsar Nicholas Wilhelm was able to escape by sacrificing his life. He would die in 1941, while living in exile in German-occupied Netherlands. Hitler was planning to take him to Berlin to be buried in a state funeral however, the former kaiser declared that he would not go back home to Germany as long as the monarchy was restored.

The abdication didn't bring about the restoration of the monarchy. Germany was declared as a republic twice: first, by The Social Democrat Chairman of the Reichstag and later with the more extreme Marxists both on the 9th of November. In the course of their campaign, Social Democrats formed an alliance with the military as well as the German upper classes , and Ebert was appointed chancellor. The extreme Marxists that were supported from the Bolsheviks of Russia or Spartacists, as they were known and were brutally suppressed. This was how Germany was spared what was the case in Bolshevik Russia. A new constitution was enacted into effect on August 11, 1919 and with Ebert as the president. It was the Weimar Republic, so-called after the town where the constitution was written would last 14 turbulent years, and would end with the advent of the Nazis' Third Reich.

On the 8th of November one day prior to the kaiser's 'abdication' made public, a group of German officials met with Allied partners in the form of a train stationed on a track located in the Forest of Compiegne - Sixty kilometers to the north of Paris.

The Germans were given an agenda of demands and only given seventy hours to think about the demands. There was no chance of negotiations. The demands had either accepted, or war would go on. The Germans signed the agreement at 5.00 am on the 11th of November. But the fighting wouldn't end till 11.00 am. For six hours, following an utterly useless butchery lasting over four decades, perhaps the worst ineffective bullets continued to be fired. Ten thousand people were killed during the period. The head of the German delegation, Matthias Erzberger, had demanded that the fighting cease immediately. The general in charge of US forces General Pershing replied that there can be no end to this conflict as long as Germany gets to its knees.'

The last soldier to die in active service during the conflict included Henry Gunther, a US private who was killed at 10.59 60 seconds prior to when the Armistice became effective.

Treaty of Versailles Treaty of Versailles

As the soldiers fought on The announcement that the Armistice was welcomed with enthusiastic celebrations across the globe. People danced and hugged on street corners, shouted, and opened champagne bottles. Church bells rang. However, on the front after 11.00 the bells did not ring. There were no celebrations. They were tired, devoid of joy, and then was reduced to a sombre silence.

There was peace however a final agreement had to be agreed on. The decision was to be taken by the Allies however, and Germany could only make one choice to make either to accept the decisions or not. The now-infamous Treaty of Versailles was signed on the 28th of June 1919 five years following the assassination attempt on the archduke of Austria-Hungary, which started the First World War.

The French were in favor of the restoration of Alsace-Lorraine , and ensures that Germany will never again pose an issue. This would mean the disarmament of Germany and the establishment of a buffer state near the Rhine River. The latter was not reached agreement on, but the Rhineland was made into an area in which German military activities could be conducted. France also wanted reparations to get paid out by Germany. In the simplest terms, France wanted the utter humiliation of Germany.

Britain did not suffer in the same way as France as well as its Empire overseas were being sacked. They did not then to insist on reparations. Also, they were not willing to accept a degraded Germany. The British most concerned about the economy of the country, hoped for the return of trade with an ad-hoc Germany.

Woodrow Wilson likewise opposed harsh treatment and was a staunch supporter of the Fourteen Points. He wanted to restore world peace on the basis of these. Most importantly was his desire to establish an effective international body that could ensure peace. France nevertheless insisted on the degrading of Germany. As the French convinced Britain to accept that Germany was to be destroyed, Wilson reluctantly agreed.

The Treaty was executed in the luxurious Hall of Mirrors at the Palace of Versailles, to show the power of France over defeated Germany. It took away Germany of large areas of territory, which included the Alsace-Lorraine region and areas that comprised Prussia and Silesia that were given to the state of Poland as well as Germany's overseas colonies as well as the Saar region near the French border , which contained precious coal mines, and the smaller Eupen-Malmedy region that was given to Belgium. Furthermore that province, Schleswig was removed by Denmark (long in the days before conflict) was returned to Denmark following a plebiscite in 1920. Germany has renounced the gains it had made through in the Treaty of Brest-Litovsk. In total, Germany has lost an area of 65000 square kilometers of land and the population of seven million.

The German army was reduced by one million and it was not able to expand any further. The navy was also reduced to only six battleships.

The most famous clause in the treaty was. 231: "Germany accepts the liability of Germany and its allies for all the damage and loss to they have caused to the Allied and Associated governments have been afflicted due to the war that was imposed on these governments by Germany along with its allies.' (italics mine)

The 'war guilt' clause obliged Germany to pay an amount of 33 million US dollars. This amounts to close to five hundred and eighty-two billion in current dollars that is more than double what the GDP per year of the United States in modern times. The reparations payments hampered Germany's economy. German industry until their eliminated through Adolf Hitler in 1933. Following World War II reparations continued at a minimum in the form of tokens. The last installment was paid on the 3rd of October, 2010.

The amount to the extent to which Germany was at fault for the war is a long-running topic of debate. Some historians have questioned the wisdom of transferring all responsibility to Germany. In the end, it was Austria-Hungary that fired the initial shots. However, Serbia seemed determined to destroy the Habsburg Empire and Russia was unable to stop Serbia. Russia did not take advantage of the chance to stay out of conflict with Germany and Germany along with Britain. Of all the powerhouses, France seems to have taken the lead in defending itself against an the threat of. Yet, it spurred Russia towards Austria - Hungary, knowing that war with Germany was likely to ensue. And Britain was quick to come to aid defenceless Belgium however, decided not to facilitate peace between the two powers. Did Britain want war too? The debate is sure to continue. One thing that these debates will demonstrate repeatedly is that there aren't winners or losers, there are no "good" or "bad" guys' in a conflict.

It was reported that the German public was furious at the time that it was announced that the Treaty is signed. Some members of Reichstag protested.

People protested in the streets. Germany had lost 10 per cent of the territory. It lost almost thirteen percent of its population, 16 percent of its coal and forty eight percent from its iron.

George Clemenceau, the Prime Minister of France was also dissatisfied by the Treaty not because it was not severe enough. The Premier minister of Great Britain, David Lloyd-George was of the opinion that the treaty was too harsh, even though Britain had gained several of Germany's colonies and predicted another war in the next twenty-five years (World War II started in 1939, just twenty years after the treaty was signed).

Woodrow Wilson, perhaps the most idealistic of those who signed the Treaty (perhaps because the United States had lost the most and had the smallest in the way of gains) was deeply dissatisfied. He had imagined the creation of a new world in accordance with its Fourteen Points. It was clear that the Treaty of Versailles seemed based on revenge, not the true wish for a permanent peace. The right to self-determination was been given lip service through this Treaty and Wilson's peace-keeping body was set up. This was known as the League Nations, a forerunner of the United States. Initially, the League was successful, but it was ultimately unsuccessful to stop an outbreak of the Second World War. In the end, however, the United States Congress, dominated by Wilson's Republican opponents, did not accept the Treaty as did it was never ratified, and the United States never became a part to the League. It is possible to say that the Treaty of Versailles literally incapacitated the president. In 1920, following an exhausting tour to help promote the Treaty the president collapsed and suffered stroke. He did not recover. He died in 1924.

History has demonstrated that Versailles was a disaster in what was supposed to be the primary goal of the Treaty which was to preserve the peace.

Austria along with Hungary were incorporated into The Treaty of Saint - Germain in 1920. Austria lost Tyrol as well as it lost the Adriatic areas in Istria, Trieste and parts of Dalmatia to Italy. The ethnically German Austria was not allowed to join Germany (it did it at the time of 1933). In 1933, the Treaty of Trianon gave Transylvania which was home to the ethnic Romanians into the kingdom of Romania. Other areas of Hungary were transferred to the newly formed States of Czechoslovakia and Serbia which was later renamed part of the kingdom of Yugoslavia ('South Slavia'). The division of territories was not always in accordance with the boundaries of ethnicity. The Treaty included thirty percent which is more than 3 million of ethnic Hungarians not within the boundaries of Hungary within Hungary itself. These differences became the source of the tensions to come within Balkan Peninsula. Balkan Peninsula.

The Treaty of Neuilly dealt with Bulgaria in 1919. Bulgaria was required to surrender a portion areas of the territory it occupied to Greece, Yugoslavia and Romania. In contrast to Germany, Austria and Hungary the reigning dynasty lasted under the Tsar Boris III.

The Treaty of Sevres, signed on 10 August 1920, addressed the Ottoman Empire. According to the provisions in the Treaty the Empire was stripped of its territory non-ethnically Turkish. The lands were put under directives from the League of Nations. They became provinces from France as well as Britain. France was granted Syria as well as Lebanon. Britain was in the control over Palestine as well as Mesopotamia (which was later transformed into modern-day Iraq). Furthermore, that the Treaty of Sevres gave European Turkey with the exception of Constantinople as well as the Greek-speaking zone that was around Izmir (called Izmir by the Greeks Smyrna) in Greece. Turkey has been divided into three zones that influenced each other: Italian as well as French within the southern hemisphere, British in Kurdistan which included Constantinople along with the Dardanelles under the control of the international community. Armenia located in west was an independent nation.

From all of the agreements, Sevres may be the one most stringent in its territorial requirements and also the most blatantly predatory. The Allied powers had started creating their own Ottoman Empire up in 1915. But, unlike their previous allies they Turks refused to sign Sevres. They joined the Turkish National Movement, led by Mustafa Kemal, defeated the troops of the occupying force and imposed an agreement, The Treaty of Laussanne that was signed with behalf of the Allied power in 1923. Kemal was named Ataturk ('Father of the Turks') by his people, ended the Ottoman Sultanate and established an independent nation called Turkey which we recognize now. Turkey may have emerged from the warafter a lengthy fighting, more powerful and stable than its previous allies. Although Germany, Austria, Hungary and Bulgaria did not manage to stay out of internal conflict in war, during the Second World War, Turkey was neutral to the end of the war and continued to fight any challenges to the territorial integrity of its country, without having to fight.

The cost is a matter of counting it.

World War II far exceeded World War I in terms losses to life, limbs and property. It was the Great War however brought the terrible devastation of conflict to the entire world in an manner it has never before experienced. As the days, weeks months, and years passed by, horror and shock transformed into gloom, despair and an eerie feeling. An entire generation had been slaughtered. The exact price for the lives of those killed in the Great War will probably never be revealed. Nearly twelve million died on the battlefield. This averages up to six thousand per day. Twenty million people were injured. More than two million civilians were killed in the military or by atrocities. Then in Belgium German military executed up to six thousands of civilians. Many more died as refugees. The Ottoman Empire murdered one million Armenians which was one of the most bloody genocides of the modern age. Certain atrocities were perpetrated by Allies as well. They also committed atrocities against the Russian Empire deported thousands of German civilians and many died in the brutal conditions.

France lost more than one million seven hundred thousand. It was the largest loss suffered by those of the Great Powers, taken as an amount of population. Russia was the most impacted. loss, averaging more than three million. Of the major belligerents, it was the United States suffered the least loss of one hundred seventeen thousand. This was because the United States had of course been fighting for only 18 months.

There was a time when the British as well as the French were in a position to recruit the troops of the colonies they had in Africa and Africa, the Americas as well as Oceania. Many of these soldiers were fighting for causes they were not familiar with, and for nations they'd never seen or take a keen interest in. The colonies contributed significantly in the fight for freedom, sometimes in a way that was not proportional to their population. Australia was one example. had more than sixty thousand casualties out of the midst of a population of just five million.

In the casualty list, we should also count nurses who are on either side.

In terms of pure material, the war cost between two 8 billion dollars US which was far in excess of the actual reparations sought by Germany along with its allies. Every major power, except in the case of United States - was burdened by debt. Inflation was widespread. In 1923, in Germany bread was priced at 428 billion marks in a period when one US dollars was valued at nearly 4 trillion dollars. There was not enough work for soldiers who returned from battlefields. This set the stage towards The Great Depression of 1929.

A few people managed to earn money from the war, including arms producers, financial institutions which loaned money to governments, as well as manufacturers of products that contributed for the war effort.

The chaotic aftermath of the war led to a variety of outbreaks of illness such as the famous 1918 influenza pandemic that swept all over the world. Influenza alone killed between 50 to 100 million in a span of five years. This was nearly one-fifth of population in just two years. Tragically, the majority who died were children.

The "war that ended all wars' as Wilson declared in the Great War, did little to bring tranquility to Europe and around the globe. In fact it planted the seeds of rivalry, discontent and hatred that would set to the fascist dictatorships of the 1930s. The year 1919 was the month that, just three years following the time that Germany was a signatory to the Treaty of Versailles, one Adolf Hitler, who had worked in the War and was now working as a member of the intelligence services was ordered to join the small Munich group called the German Workers Party. Much like the majority of Germans, Hitler hated the Treaty and was terribly affronted by the humiliation of Germany. He noticed his way to the German Worker's Party shared his personal views on what was to come for Germany. It was militaristic, nationalist and anti-Semitic. It was the reason he joined it. After a short time, the party change its name, it became"the National Socialist German Workers Party and Hitler created its symbol which was the Swastika.

Conclusion

In the days before that the Treaty of Versailles was even signed before the Treaty of Versailles was signed, the German citizens were aware that the word "defeat" was scrawled across the wall. As the German military was splintering in the front, German civic society was in decline at home. In October 1918, a local rebellion called"the "Revolution between 1918 and 1919" was triggered. The leaders were mostly of unions and other workers groups that held protests within factories, as well as in other industry areas.

In the beginning the uprisings appeared to be similar to the revolutions which took place in Russia just prior to when the communists took control. It's rather ironic think about how the pressure of Germany was instrumental in triggering (and certain people even actively promote) this Russian collapse that resulted in Russia becoming the state of communism and then to see Germany to follow the same route.

The change of Germany to an Marxist government was something in which communists both in Germany as well as Russia had been keenly taking part in. Germany was, after all, was the home for Karl Marx himself, and the Marxist's communist hens were finally coming home to lay their eggs. But the opposition was aware to the plight German society was falling into, and frightened of the same fate as Russia A hefty political opposition was forged.

The so-called moderates urged the most conservative parts in German society to lead the way against the radical left-leaning socialists who came from trade unions. In the final analysis, the moderates won out, and instead of becoming a communist state, Germany was to evolve into an parliamentary democracy, also that was referred to as"the "Weimer Republic."

The truth is that this republic was at risk of failing as well in the event that Nazi fascists under Adolf Hitler hijacked it a few decades later. But, the state of affairs improved following the demise from the Kaiser Wilhelm II in the early months of November. Germany declared that it was now an interim government that had enough grit in order to negotiate an armistice deal in conjunction with Allies on 11 November 1918.

The initial agreement was an agreement to cease fire that required the Germans acknowledge defeat and cease hostilities. The agreement was merely a promise with no other conditions than the immediate cessation or end of combat. After a meeting at the Palace of Versailles in France and the Germans would have to confront the harsh conditions that the Allies were expecting them to accept.

The treaty basically declared Germany morally responsible for any damages which it had incurred from other European nations it opposed, and required the bankrupt nation to make reparations to pay back.

It also forced Germany to reduce its military presence as other nations were allowed to expand their arsenals around the German state and even build military bases on German territory, for instance located in the

Rhine region that lies between France as well as Germany.

Initially, Germans did not want to sign it. However, after a long discussion the decision was made that Germany could not choose. The Germans determined that if they did not accept these terms, the Allies could be tempted to invading Germany as they knew that the German military was in any way equipped to stop an enormous force of invasion.

However, that signing treaty will leave a bitterness which will be a major factor in the destruction of Germany in the following two years, until the situation was so toxic that it led to the rise of Hitler as well as the Nazis. There has been a debate that, even though this Treaty of Versailles was viewed as the end of the war, it was actually just the beginning of an much more horrific conflict to come.

www.ingramcontent.com/pod-product-compliance
Lightning Source LLC
Chambersburg PA
CBHW050026130526
44590CB00042B/1927